MODEL IN PARIS

MODEL IN PARIS

Valerie Thurlow

ROBERT HALE · LONDON

© Valerie Thurlow 1975
First published in Great Britain 1975

ISBN 0 7091 5050 4

Robert Hale & Company
Clerkenwell House
Clerkenwell Green
London EC1R 0HT

Composed by Specialised Offset Services Ltd
and printed and bound in Great Britain by
Redwood Burn Limited, Trowbridge & Esher

CONTENTS

ILLUSTRATIONS

"Gu Mo Mhathair Ghradhach"

1

GIRL FROM ESSEX

The day of the audition, the butterflies nearly flew away with me. It was warm, sunny June in Paris, the chestnuts in full regalia, as Felicity and I stepped from a taxi in the Rue Francois I.

I was, however, feeling anything but warm and sunny inside. I had what the French call *le traque*, which means roughly that I had butterflies in the tummy. Here I was, a typical English Miss from a small town in Essex, England, daring to compete for one of the most glamorous jobs in the world, that of top model with the world-famous couturier Pierre Balmain, and my hands were cold and clammy and my nose was shining like a beacon.

As a matter of fact, if I had known that my slinky parade up and down the runway at the audition would give rise to such hilarity and mirth from *le Maestro* himself, I swear I would never have made it through that elegant gold-plated front door.

Felicity, to my further consternation, did not seem to be at all perturbed by the ordeal, and I noticed to my horror that she was even nonchalantly chewing gum.

I had spent the entire morning on my appearance; fixing my long blonde hair into an elaborately simple chignon, trying (as I thought) to capture 'the image', and finally dressing myself in my best navy-blue suit, with the blue-and-white check inset pleats, that I had bought last year at a

Harrods' sale. By covering my face with the palest of make-up and fixing on two pairs of extra-long eyelashes, to give that moth-eyed look, I had tried hard to obliterate my healthy girl-next-door look, and to cultivate a little decadent sophistication. So I really did not think that my appearance deserved such a hilarious reception.

But as we climbed the dove-coloured staircase to the upper salon and asked to speak to the boss (my policy always — a sort of nervous precosity), I had no idea as yet of the reaction I would get.

A blue-grey lady in black, jangling with a twenty-four-carat manner and real gold jewellery, asked us to wait whilst she looked for the *chef de cabine*, whatever that was. (My French was rather rudimentary at that stage, to say the least.) We sat in silence beneath a portrait of an elegant Edwardian duchess, with a stare which matched that of the *vendeuses* or sales women, who were busily passing to and fro. The atmosphere was surprisingly informal even though there was that exclusive smell of Balmain's Vent Vert perfume wafting through the air. The *vendeuses* chattered like grasshoppers, and one of them even smiled at me.

A messenger boy appeared carrying an enormous bouquet of pink roses saying that they were for *Mademoiselle Cassandre*; obviously one of the mannequins I thought, not a little enviously, and tried to imagine myself becoming so exotic. I concluded finally that much depends on your point of view. An English girl is probably just as exotic to the French as vice versa, I told myself.

Just then the *chef de cabine* appeared. This is the woman in charge of the *cabine*, which is the name given to the dressing room where the mannequins sit preparing themselves, and where all the priceless clothes are hung. A *cabine des mannequins* is the collective term for a group of mannequins, rather as one refers to a string of race-horses, or a pride of lions — or a clowder of cats. She was hard and bitchy looking, with dark glasses and a bright scarlet mouth, one word from which was guaranteed to curdle even the bluest of blood. She showed us into a stifling dungeon, with mirrors all round in which I was able to observe my hot perspiring face next to the mustard-yellow tweed suit that she gave me to try on; it was a disaster with my blonde hair. Then she departed in search of Monsieur Eric.

Felicity had fared better, with a red wool dress which suited her dark hair and eyes. After she had fastened it up and nonchalantly lit a cigarette, we decided that she must have got it on back to front, as there was no room for her bosom, so we undid it and turned it round. But since this way seemed even worse, we concluded that it must have been made on a boy of thirteen, and that the best thing for her to do was to keep her arms still, her shoulders rounded and her chest caved in. This was rather hard for Felicity who had once been Miss Margate.

Monsieur Eric was a tall, handsome, enigmatic Dane. He scarcely seemed to glance at us before asking me to parade before him, up and down a short runway with rows of fragile little gold chairs on either side. He sat stoney-faced as I stepped through the curtains and went through my ordeal. I didn't feel at all like me in the yellow suit, and wished like mad that I could stop and explain to him that I couldn't bear the colour. But I didn't dare; and besides, a good manne-quin's job is to make anything look absolutely fabulous, from a diamond tiara to a flour sack. So I pretended that it was the most gorgeous thing I had ever set eyes on and that everyone must want at least a dozen like it instantly. Luckily the next thing that they picked out for me to try was a smart little black dress trimmed with ostrich feathers and gleaming wickedly with sequins, which simply shrieked of Paris. It had a plunging back and once again no bosom (fortunately I don't have Felicity's problem), and I felt good in it.

Maggie, the *chef*, kept up a long tirade of impatience for

no apparent reason at all, of which I understood less than nothing. Once again I made my entrance through the drapes. I stepped out briskly walking quickly, toes down first, spun round twice at the foot of the runway, no smile, hoping Monsieur Eric would not notice the tremor of my ankle as I turned, walked up and down once more, and finally swept off, feeling just like a filly at a horse sale.

'I wonder if he would like to feel my fetlocks and examine my teeth', I thought somewhat ruefully as I changed once again, this time into a long slinky cut-on-the-cross 1930-style evening dress, with large brown-and-white flowers printed on silk crêpe. It was lovely and droopy, with a long stole round the neck and hanging down the back; the kind of dress for wearing on the terrace at a summer party *chez vous* in Monte Carlo, and that Gertrude Lawrence might have worn in Noel Coward's *Private Lives*. Of course one really had to be an absolute bus ticket to wear it, and I slunk onto the podium holding everything in, and swinging the stole nonchalantly over one shoulder.

It was then that I heard it. The laughter I mean. A loud peal of it, followed by a stream of something in French. Realising that this must be Monsieur Balmain himself I turned cold and hot, spun round, and prepared to beat a Waterloo-style retreat out of the salon, vowing to look for a job as a dairy-maid or whatever else instead. I was not going to be laughed at!

I had got as far as the exit when I heard, 'Come back here *ma cherie*'. I stopped dead and the *patron* beckoned me to him.

He was round and tanned with rather gentle eyes, and seemed very international. He looked much more like a business tycoon than a dress-designer. Which, of course, in a sense he is. Such a rare combination of business sense and artistic talent could hardly fail to add up to the sort of success that Pierre Balmain has. He now eyed me up and down.

'You have such a bizarre walk', he said comfortingly. 'Obviously you've been a dancer.'

Blushingly I admitted that it was true. Seven years of classical ballet training plus two years in the profession were bound to show. Apparently I turn my toes out, arch my instep, and lean backwards. I walk very quickly too. Working in London, my dancer's walk had often been criticised. I soon learned that the *haute couture* adores such eccentricities.

He eyed me up and down.

'Hm, an interesting English girl. I shall call you "Lady Bread and Butter".'

Suddenly he grabbed hold of my carefully arranged chignon, flattened the top, and dragged it back behind my ears muttering, 'Petite tête, petite tête!' Then turning to Monsieur Eric he said, 'Cut off most of her hair and have the rest dyed black. Heads are going to be small this season'.

And with that he swept out, leaving me open-mouthed and loose at the hinges. Astounded would perhaps be the *le bon mot.* 'Lady Bread and Butter' was about to be cut, wrapped and served up to the most elegant customers in the world.

Monsieur Eric drew me aside then, and became much more human as he explained that the fittings commenced at the beginning of July and lasted for one month. The money that *couture* houses pay their mannequins is scarcely enough to keep a flea dressed in velvet, but what the job lacks financially it makes up for in many other ways. All the mannequins are able to choose for themselves an expensive model gown from the collection, they travel to the most exotic places, stay at luxury hotels, and once the fittings are over they have only to show the collection from three until four o'clock each day. Thus there is plenty of time to make one's fortune from photographs and publicity.

Me and all my butterflies were unanimous. I accepted: But what about Felicity?

'Tell your girl-friend that we are looking for a blonde,' suggested Eric gently. It wasn't true, but I liked him for caring about other people's feelings enough to tell the white lie. Every fashion house has its own particular style of manne-quin and is careful to engage only those in keeping with its particular mystic. Thus Felicity was engaged by the House of Lanvin that very same afternoon. They adored her coltish gait and Sophia Loren-ish allure. So we were both of us overjoyed as we celebrated on the terrace *au Deux Magots* that evening, and congratulated each other through a haze of Pernod.

'Blimey! Wait'll I tell me Mum', said Felicity, lapsing into her native Cockney, overcome by sheer seventy-per-cent-proof emotion. Very soon, we were perhaps to find ourselves amongst the best-dressed and most sought-after women in the world, with half the noblemen of Europe fighting for our telephone numbers — if only we could afford to get a telephone laid on.

My family was *boulversé* by the news. But then they have always been totally in favour of anything I have ever wanted to do, however crack-brained it may have seemed to them. Sometimes my ideas had been little more than whims, and had cost us money which we could ill afford. But early ballet lessons, drama classes, horse-show jumping etc., etc. — they had approved of it all and had always given me terrific and enthusiastic support.

We used to live in a small village in the Midlands, and on those rare occasions when my parents took my elder sister and me into town, it was almost invariably to the ballet. On one of these occasions I had the great good fortune to meet the Russian ballerina Hélène Armfelt. It was after a perform-ance of *Swan Lake*, at the Birmingham Theatre Royal, and we had gone backstage to congratulate her; her dancing had been original and ecstatic. She proved to be even more original and out-of-this-world in the flesh than she had been on stage. From being merely friends of friends we subsequently became very close, and she would often come and stay with us, hanging her tights out on our washing line and darning the toes of her pink satin ballet shoes (not because they had holes in them but to prevent slipping on stage), and she really became one of the family.

Our home was a little cottage which was all sideways and was apparently subsiding very gradually into an extinct salt-mine. Hélène loved the place, and each time upon arrival she would incline her head at a forty-five-degree angle, hang her tongue out, and roar with laughter. The cottage didn't mind, it could take a joke; it had had three-hundred-odd years of existence in which to become accustomed to its deformity. We all loved the place.

Sometimes Hélène would practise her *adagio* or do some *barre* work in the garden, whilst my mother yodelled her native Scottish miscellany from the kitchen. My father, an ex ship's radio-officer who had joined the B.B.C. way back in its infancy, adored Hélène. He was now learning Russian, and used to hold long painful conversations with her over tea. (With milk of course.)

Until then, my passion had been horses. We lived in horsy country, so my sister Diana and I spent most of our time fox-hunting, going to horse-shows and mucking out stables. As a matter of fact, so strong was my early passion for horses that I had even planned some day to marry one. But meeting Hélène changed all that, and ballet became my life from then on. It was to stand me in good stead in later years.

I pirouetted, *pas de chat*-ed and *grande jete*-d my way through seven years of ballet training, until the day when I failed an audition for the Royal Ballet School. It was the worst day of my life. The reason was simple; at twelve years old I had the same elongated stature that I have today, being at the time five feet nine inches in my tights, and though the *haute couture* business may adore freaks, the ballet world prefers them in miniature. I must have cried for a week.

At school I began to suffer agonies from corny nicknames, and developed a kind of stoop to cover my embarrassment; this too turned out to be an asset later on. Being tall I was expected to be good at games, and essential to the hockey team. They soon discovered how much I cared about hockey, a thoroughly brutal and beastly game. I prefer the milder kinds of sport such as horse-riding or sailing, where something other than my own legs does the conveying. Fundamentally, let's face it, I suppose I am lazy. Not to mention my instinct for survival.

When it came to educating us my family was always ready to find the funds somehow and 'afford it later', as my mother used to say. Like the time I've already mentioned when I decided to be an actress. I was sixteen, and just leaving school. The family had dutifully tried to encourage me into some sensible, stable profession (father even suggested I.B.M. at one point) but I kept insisting on fairyland. I hated reality and badly needed magic and glitter and glamour. I have never stopped believing in fairy stories, and I never shall. So, the theatre being the nearest thing to my world, an audition was arranged for the famous Royal Academy of Dramatic Art.

Miraculously they accepted me, plus my rendering of excerpts from *Alice in Wonderland* and *Lady Windermere's Fan*. There remained only the problem of how to pay the fees. Father examined his bank balance, and shook his head sadly; my mother reluctantly agreed, and we all gazed gloomily at one another. And then my grandfather shuffled out of his room wearing his old tartan slippers, and pressed something into my hand. It was thirty pounds, enough to pay for the first term. It was a good part of his savings. Even though a 'show biz' career was far from what he, an army veteran, would have considered wise, he nevertheless wouldn't dream of seeing me turn down a dream of my own. I cried as I hugged him gratefully. Dear old man!

But after an abortive six months at R.A.D.A., where I slept

My very first professional photograph

An early job as a photographic model

through forty-two lectures on 'The History of the Theatre', I developed an embarrassing stammer in diction class, and literally fainted with fright during the end-of-term production of *Crime and Punishment* (I suppose I am what is known as an introverted extrovert). I came, one day, to the joyous conclusion that my calling was to the world of fine art. It was a wonderful release.

'A painter I will be', I sang to myself as I enrolled at the Regent Street Polytechnic (The Poly) to study art and to specialise in theatrical design. What a fabulous three years I passed, studying, learning, making beautiful friendships and going to student parties and jazz clubs. I had grown my wings at long last.

Three of us, myself, my cousin Penny and my best friend Gay, also art students, shared an apartment together in Belgravia (a very posh address. I can't think why it had such a low rent). We were all so desperately poor that we lived on brown rice, which cost one shilling a packet and lasted for days, occasionally mixed with an onion as a special treat. Gay had bought a whole string of onions for five bob from a Breton on a bicycle. (The Bretons come over every year, on the ferry-boat from Brittany, and cycle to London to sell, or literally peddle, their onions around the streets.) One day I noticed that we all appeared to be getting 'slit eyes' and yellow patches. Penny immediately diagnosed our complaint as scurvy, so in true limey fashion I went out and bought some limes to restore our English roses!

Often we used to scrounge breakfast off Old Joe the night-watchman, who was 'minding an 'ole in the road' in Regent Street. Joe was convinced he was the reincarnation of Rembrandt. His leathery face, long hair, floppy hat and kerchief were identical, even if his talents as a painter were not. But he cooked fabulous bacon-and-eggs over a brazier in the middle of the road, whilst the morning rush-hour traffic narrowly missed us.

After three years of rice with the occasional porridge sandwich, and now and then dinner in a restaurant with one of our respective (and respected) fathers, I became restless again, and aware that there was a whole wealth of even more exciting things going on in the world that I knew nothing about. Everyone but me, it seemed, had beautiful clothes and shoes, everyone but me was able to travel the big wide world, everyone but me knew the taste of champagne, had seen the ruins of the Acropolis by moonlight, eaten sharks' fins and ridden in a gondola. (Actually I still haven't come to that one.) The men in my life were practically non-existent, and those who did materialise were far from suave or sophisticated. Callow youths you might call them. My cousin Penny now, she always had lots of boy-friends. She has a taste for the insane, plus a gigantic sense of humour which always seems to attract them like mad. We differ in that I am basically rather a shy person, though at the same time somewhat ego-based. For instance, I am never attracted to a man unless he is attracted to me first; and also, if I walk into a party and see a fabulous-looking man, the last thing I will do is take any notice of him. Occasionally this approach pays off, but more often than not, he is snapped up by some less retiring female. *C'est la guerre!* as they say.

But one day Penny came home and told me about the most fabulous creature she had met in the doctor's waiting room up in Hampstead. Apparently he was tall and Grecian looking.

'He looks exactly like that statue of Caesar Augustus in the British Museum', she breathed ecstatically. We were studying the Ancient Greeks and Romans at that time. According to her description he had thick curly hair, a perfectly classical bone-structure, and large soul-piercing green eyes. He lived on an ex-motor-torpedo-boat on the Thames, together with a German shepherd dog called Sally, and he was, what's more, a penniless poet. His name was Michael.

Some days later we chanced to meet when he came to our home. He was everything she had described, and those mystical grey-green eyes had such humour in their gaze. Far be it from me to poach on someone else's property, but I couldn't help a feeling of excitement at our meeting and each subsequent one. It was like meeting an old familiar friend. There was never any need to explain anything that we said, for all was automatically understood. It was just like talking to *me*. One night, a group of us were drinking wine around the stove on board the boat. I had walked up on deck to get some air and watch the dawn coming up. Suddenly I came face-to-face with Michael. I started to turn away shyly, but he laid a hand on my arm.

'When I look at you, it's like kissing you', he said simply and seriously.

That finished me, I couldn't help it. A rocket went up in my heart and burst into a thousand fragments. However after that I didn't see him for some time. Neither did Penny. Then one afternoon we ran into each other in the street. We walked home together and giggled on the way about the poet John Betjemen, and recited Dylan Thomas to each other, and pitied the poor people of Surbiton (an endless London suburb) who knew not freedom like ours. By then, Penny had fallen for a clarinet player with the Temperance Seven (a sort of rock group), and Michael and I began to see a lot more of each other. Then, one afternoon, he came to meet me at the Poly. As we wandered along Regent Street, he stopped suddenly and said to me out of the blue, 'Val, I'm going to Paris next week. I am going to start an English-language theatre there. Come with me!'

It's hard to describe the emotions I went through then; I was thrilled and devastated at the same time. The only trouble was that around this time I had been making a few drastic decisions regarding my own career. I had a craving for the unfamiliar, the exotic. It seemed to me that everyone I

knew had had at least three love affairs and was either
married, divorced or living in sin. And I? Up to then all I had
had was a mad crush on an English-master at school. What
kind of a woman of the world was I? I wanted to be someone
like the people I had read about in books. Having completed
three years of studies, I had concluded that the career of a
poverty-stricken artist was not for me. I find it hard to
abstract myself when I am hungry, although at art school we
had always consoled ourselves with the thought that hunger
sharpens the intellect. And besides, what did I have to paint?
I knew nothing. I needed to stir things up for myself; I
needed above all, the freedom to do so. Perhaps in order to
discover oneself, one has to discover who one is not.

I was at least a little mixed-up as I tried to explain to
Michael why I could not go to Paris with him. Perhaps the
reason was simply that he was an ascetic, and I was caught up
with exploring earthbound pleasures. A number nineteen bus
drew up then and impulsively I jumped aboard. As I stood on
the platform and watched the gap between us widening as the
bus pulled away I saw his eyes looking into me still, and I
knew that even though we should not meet again for a long,
long time, somewhere down in my deepest heart I loved him.
He was my soul companion.

But I had made my decision; to get out and learn from the
school of life. As the bus bore me away it seemed a fitting
send off.

2

"TALK OF THE TOWN"

A few weeks later, taking my courage in both hands I walked into the bank, opened an account, smiled sweetly at the bank manager and, just to put him at his ease, asked him for an overdraft. He in turn gave me the once over, then the twice over, smiled showing his teeth, and then nodded slowly. The nodding continued for some time, until eventually I fumbled my way out of the bank armed with £50 and the first real financial proof of my charm. It was a lesson I was never to forget — how to exploit your potential. I had become aware that the relationship between men and women is older than business, and my youth gave me the courage to give it a try.

For the past month I had not had two halfpennies to rub together and now I felt just like Barbara Hutton, so I went straight to the most expensive hairdresser I could find and had my hair dyed pink, just for the hell of it.

I had no idea what I was going to do; and then one day I ran into Janice, an old friend who introduced me to twenty-three-year-old Colin. He was looking for two girls to team up with Janice as a glamorous trio, and had magnificent future plans for us in show business doing West End and international cabaret, with of course a large cut for himself. He offered glittering visions of Las Vegas, and millions of dollars rolling in, and retirement at an early age. It sounded marvellous. There was just one snag however. He required us to sing, and in harmony if possible. We thought about it for a long time, about fifteen seconds, and agreed to give it a whirl. We quickly found another girl who had the same essential attributes as ourselves, being tall, blonde, breadless and brimming with optimism. Her name was Sylvia and she was a dancer with the Crazy Gang Show at the Victoria Palace. We decided to call ourselves 'The Mayfair Kittens', and began about three weeks of rehearsals. Now, though it may be hard to muster a battalion of troops on time, one would imagine it would not be so difficult to organise three girls; but Colin had his work cut out in trying to get three star-struck egos into one place simultaneously. Also, each of us had a different image of how we should sound as a group. Janice wanted harmony like the Beach Boys, Colin had the Beverly/Andrews Sisters in mind and I wanted us to have a message. Sylvia just hummed gaily along with things.

Eventually Colin arranged several auditions for us, including one with a well-known West End nightclub called The Bagatelle. The day before the audition I went to bed with flu and a raging fever. I still shared a flat with my cousins Penny and Sandy who had a somewhat morbid interest in medicine and were very sympathetic. They had me over the sink inhaling Friar's Balsam for my delicate throat and then proceeded to pile blankets and eiderdowns onto my bed so that I should 'sweat it out'. Not a very glamorous situation for a budding star singer. I sniffed.

The following day, in a drenching London mist that would have caused Noah to put up the shutters on his Ark and start a wet fish shop instead, I staggered along to the nightclub. Colin was waiting for us in the foyer apparently feeling more nervous than we were. While we were waiting for the final countdown to our cataclysmic launch into the 'big-time', he paced up and down the narrow passage outside the manager's office, practically biting our fingernails, whilst ranting on about how shoddy we looked and couldn't we at least have got some sleep before coming along. 'And what about your hair?' he screamed at me. When I consider this remark, in fact he had a point. It had been dyed and re-dyed until by this time it was really quite dead. Not just blonde, but colourless and broken, it hung from the crown of my head like a sort of limp bedraggled halo.

The manager, very Jewish and business-like, twitched slightly in the dark when we went into our act and after what must have seemed to him a great display of patience muttered, rather disagreeably I thought, 'You've got the looks girls, but-er – that singing . . . a little less singing and a little more dancing. And-er – those dresses. Get rid of them!' It seemed to us that he wanted strippers, not a trio of would-be Beverly Sisters; however, this was not the case. He merely wanted to exchange our voices for our legs, and to have a little less covering upon what he was offering his customers with their dinner. We compromised and agreed; that is Colin compromised, and we agreed. From Bermans the theatrical costumiers we ordered three sexy, shocking pink, sequinned leotards which had seen better days, and we got the job.

We lasted exactly six days, and on the sixth the show went up late and Janice, who was doubling at the Don Juan Club, which meant that she had another show beginning at 1 o'clock, decided to up and leave in the middle of our act, so as not to miss her other gig. In fact, right bang in the middle of a number Janice took off. We were not, however, more amazed than the manager at this absence of faith. He stood there mesmerised and goggle-eyed as Janice pulled on her old brown tweed coat over her black and pink sequinned costume and made for the exit. The music stopped. Sylvia and I smiled fixedly at each other and then went into a spontaneous spasm of giggles. It was the end. After that, Colin, our nervous manager, decided that there were less trying things to do.

So it was that I found myself out of work again, and

playing cards with cousins Penny and Sandy and two dancers who lived upstairs. It was through these two dancers that I heard of a theatre show called 'Talk of the Town'. Then one day, in the *Stage* a weekly theatrical news sheet, I saw an advertisement for an audition there for dancers. The 'Talk of the Town' was and still is a theatre-restaurant doing big business.

Thousands of girls were there of all shapes and sizes, among them, I was surprised to note, a fair sprinkling of classical dancers from Sadlers Wells, the Royal Ballet and other famous schools. My mind went to my own early classical ballet training, and I hoped that it would not be necessary to compete with them on their terms. Playing cards with Penny, and my many other varied activities since then, had not exactly sharpened up my *pas de deux*. We waited around drinking coffee until eventually we were called on stage, thirty at a time, and shown a routine by a languid mauve and green choreographer. I stayed at the back and stumbled through the complicated modern dance arrangement as best I could. When my turn came to go up front, all I could see were bright lights and stoney-faced impresarios puffing their way through fat cigars, doing their C.B. Cochrane bit. I was wearing sheer black tights, and a black leotard with a plunging back and a large blood-red rose at the base of the plunge. I really think the rose did more for me than my *grante jeté*. I was chosen, along with nineteen others.

We summoned up enough between us for a magnum of champagne and it was celebration night in Dorset Square; and though since then I have seen enough champagne to refloat the old Queen Mary, I don't even remember it having tasted so good.

The show was a spectacular, extravaganza type, built around Eartha Kitt, who used to ride to the theatre every night on an ancient bicycle and appear moments later covered from head to toe with leopard skin, reclining on a couch carried on high by four boy dancers. It was 'a gas' as the saying goes. I also worked there with Sophie Tucker.

We all adored working with Lena Horne. She is married to her band-leader, Lenny Hayton. In the dressing rooms of the 'Talk of the Town' there is a loud-speaker system that relays the show from the stage and the time signals from the call-boy. I remember once the voice of Lena Horne's husband coming over the speaker saying, 'Mrs Hayton, I love you'. It was a beautiful piece of reality in a make-believe world; but then Lena Horne is a very real person.

I have always been extremely vague and absent-minded, and once the show had been rehearsed and running for a while it became very automatic, and consequently I used to turn my mind to other things and let my body perform its motions of its own accord. The inevitable happened one night during a Tahitian number. Wearing a white and turquoise sarong with flowers everywhere and ultra-violet lighting with South Sea Island music, I awoke from my trance to find myself on the wrong side of the stage and panicked. Scrambling over a whole heap of dancers on the floor doing a *grand developé*, a nightmare forest of undulating arms and legs, I finally found an exit between a pair of knees and fled to the dressing-room in tears. The audience tittered unkindly while the producer turned white with rage.

The show was one of those interminable evergreen shows, with occasional transfusions of new talent and a changing 'Top Spot' system of short-run celebrity acts. After about a year of this fun-factory life I began to get a little bored with the experience, and started searching for new outlets for my stage-struck enthusiasm. One night after the show, whilst at a show biz café, a place full of musicians between gigs, strippers between strips, and comedians between jokes, I got into conversation with a beautiful, loud, and gentle show biz queen called Janet Howes. She told me of a club called Winstons where they needed show-girls, so I took time out the following day from my daylight beauty sleep and went along to audition for them. It was another world from the brash extravaganza of the 'Talk of the Town'. Small by comparison, it nevertheless contained a gigantic aura of personality, excitement, and chic entertainment. This show was a fast-moving *Beyond the Fringe* type of revue, poking fun at current events and news. Nearly all the leads in the show, who were simultaneously appearing elsewhere on the legitimate stage, have since achieved stardom in the cinema, the West End, or on Broadway; such people as Victor Spinetti, Barbara Ferris, and Danny la Rue.

The stage was no bigger than a postage stamp, which brought one into rather intimate contact with the audience, who were on the whole regular customers and who knew the show by heart and were always 'with us'. (Which reminds me of a famous film actor, who passed out on the edge of our stage, whilst we danced around and over him.) We enjoyed our late-night frolic. It became rather like some sort of private party, and we became very sensitive to 'send ups' from the non-regulars. So when one night a group of debs with their chinless-wonder Guards-officer-type boy-friends arrived and began to shower us with ice-cubes, English upper-class arrogance, and ill-manners, we were not overjoyed to say the least. At one point in the show four other dancers and myself, led by Janet Howes, had to pass in line very close to their table. While we all sang and kept our 'eyes and teeth' smiles switched on, I suddenly heard Janet sing, 'Ready girls', a wicked gleam in her eye, and we hooked our hands under the table and tipped it up, right into their aristocratic laps. Champagne spilled everywhere, ice-cubes down décolletages, icy water in chukka boots, and on we danced. It was a glorious victory. The manager, as luck would have it, had understood the situation perfectly and was on our side.

Dear Janet Howes. This was all due to her initiative and wonderful sense of drama. We were all devastated some months later to learn of her suicide. No one had ever guessed that she of all people, so funny and gay and dedicated to show business, had shadows of this nature in her mind.

At this epoch I was very anxious to succeed in show business and would try anything for the fun of it. I had also begun to take small acting parts on B.B.C. Television, and in one play I actually played a nun. It amused me to go for costume fittings to Bermans, one day for a sexy spangled leotard and the next day for a nun's habit. It helped me to keep a flexible image of myself. It was during a television show that I met Douglas, the leader of a strange group of anarchistic musicians called 'The Alberts'. There were four of them, and they appeared on this show playing ancient musical instruments such as a one-stringed blow fiddle and a flügelhorn, Douglas himself entwined in an enormous curly euphonium, and all standing up in dustbins. He had a large red beard and a tremendous, dead-pan sense of humour. We giggled a lot on that show. He was such a gas we became good friends.

During rehearsals at the 'Talk of the Town' a few days later the call boy came to tell me that a strange gentleman was waiting to see me. I sensed an air of incredulity from him and I soon discovered the reason, for there waiting in the stage door was Douglas wearing a soldier's uniform of the 1914-18 war complete with puttees, immersed in an enormous black bearskin coat, and looking like something from an Eisenstein movie. Peering through his pince-nez he said 'I've come to take you to tea. Do you like caviar?' I'd never tasted it but of course I said I adored it. 'Come on then', he said, 'the Iron Horse is awaiting us'.

The Iron Horse turned out to be an ancient luggage van which he had bought from British Railways for £5. It had a chimney belching exhaust fumes through the roof of the cab, a female arm that shot out to indicate when it was turning left, a lavatory chain attached to a fiendishly loud Klaxon horn, and numerous odd buckets and paraphernalia hanging around underneath which added to the general clanking as we proceeded at a reckless five miles an hour round Hyde Park.

'I bought this for Jimmy', said Douglas gesturing towards the back of the van. Jimmy turned out to be a large ginger greyhound who had been cast out of the dog racing fraternity because of his strange terror of electric hares. Passing in front of Buckingham Palace the Iron Horse belched and sighed and came to a halt with smoke billowing through the floor by my feet. Douglas was prepared for this. He leapt out, grabbed one of the buckets, which was full of water, and dowsed the engine with it. After a few more hiccups and sighs we continued.

Douglas had a large, sprawling basement flat in Bayswater very like a junk shop. It was full of bits of furniture stacked one piece on top of the next, cases of stuffed birds, old clocks, phonographs and all kinds of old and rare musical instruments. The tea was served from a samovar as we sat on the floor eating delicious caviar; equally delicious, or more so, than that which I was later to sup on at Balmain's special showing for Queen Sirikit. Apart from doing various gigs and featuring in a West End Show called *An Evening of British Rubbish*, Douglas used to drive a van at night distributing newspapers to shops. One night he collected me after the show at Winstons, which finished at 3 a.m., and I rode with him on his rounds, Douglas dressed in a suit of 2-inch wide black and white stripes, somewhat like a stage convict's outfit, a panama hat, and smoking a large Havana cigar. Crazy, but I loved it.

By this time I was kept very busy indeed with two shows a night at Winstons, the perpetual Talk of the Town, and an ever-increasing number of television commitments. I was earning a steady £30 a week, and anything from £20 to £60 for a television show. Big money in pre-inflation Britain. Most of my money was spent on clothes and especially shoes, which I can never have enough of. I think they *make* an outfit. When I am a millionairess I shall have whole rooms filled with them! I used to love to walk around the shops in Knightsbridge and notice the clothes and casual chic elegance of the daughters and wives of embassy officials who seem to congregate in that area. They had that *international* look — the crocodile handbag, the Chanel suit — all the rage just then) the Gucci shoes, and armsful of jangly gold bracelets, and of course the all-year-round sun-tan. I used to think how nice it would be to travel and absorb a little of this aura. However, I was very tied up with my show biz career.

Then one night at the Talk of the Town, a young man with a pale, moody face and cameras burgeoning from every limb appeared and changed my whole life. He was taking photographs for *Life* magazine, and he squeezed into a corner of our cramped dressing-room and took some rather candid pictures of us preparing ourselves, catching me with twenty-four inches of hair round my face which I was teasing into shape.

'That's groovy', he said, and clicked the shutter sixteen times. 'How would you like to do some modelling?'

3

THE LONDON SCENE

On my way to the photographer's studio, three days later, feet not wanting to go but the address card leading me on, I thought, 'I've heard those lines before'. But I had decided to trust him even if his eyebrows did meet in the middle, my curiosity far outweighing my suspicion. Eventually I found myself climbing a dark staircase, to the tune of some far-out jazz from above, with a sinking feeling in the pit of my stomach, sweaty palms and a nervous twitch in my right eyelid. The stairs opened into a large loft, and the sound of someone sawing something metal led me over to stage left where I discovered my photographer with his pale face looking as though it had been slept in, making an excruciating noise. He appeared to be sawing a large curly Victorian bathtub in half.

'Do me a favour' he said. 'See if you can cop hold of this'. His accent was a mixture of Cockney and American. 'Perhaps you could sit in it and stop the rock whilst I saw', he suggested. So I stepped into the tub as coolly as the Queen Mother, and crouched with my handbag in my lap pretending that I knew hundreds of people who sawed bathtubs in half all the time. After some ear-splitting gyrations with the saw, the bathtub suddenly rocked into two parts and he sat back on his heels and surveyed the deed, while I stretched my feet out and lit a cigarette, with studied Hollywood elegance. 'What on earth are you going to do with it?' I finally simply

31

had to ask. 'I'm going to paint them black, line them with foam rubber, and they'll make just fantastic chairs. But first I'm going to take you like that'.

Now I had often been photographed before; in fact I had once even, during my art-school days, been 'discovered' while I was sketching in the Victoria and Albert Museum, by a photographer who asked me to pose for him wearing some fabulous, exotic jewellery from the tomb of the Pharoahs. I had desperately wanted to look sophisticated and inscrutable, and tried hard to achieve this image, but when the photos finally appeared in *The Tatler* I looked just about as exotic as Doris Day, and people tended to say things like 'Doesn't she look like her father'. So, determined to rectify this image, I straightened myself into a pose of refined elegance, and turning my good side to the camera gazed vacantly through a glassy wall of diamonds, dropping a curtain between myself and the lens, and waiting for him to tell me to watch for the flight of wild birds. It didn't take me long however to discover that this was not the way modern photographers operate at all.

'Let your hair down' he said, and I obediently undid my carefully-pinned-up beehive hairdo and shook my hair free. The shutter clicked a dozen times during this operation and he asked me all sorts of leading questions to which I was forced to react, and each time I moved the shutter clicked.

'When you work with a photographer you have to keep moving around and helping him to find shots', he told me, and I realised that the method of holding a fixed pose for twenty minutes while the lighting was arranged belonged to the Victorian era. He explained to me that modelling is very hard work, and that you have to be very professional, and always have a dozen different hair pieces, and also an ability to change your 'look' according to the clothes. A top-class agent is essential, plus an ability to arrive punctually in a studio at nine o'clock in the morning, made-up and ready to

Above. 'In the rue Francois I'. I become a Balmain mannequin
Below. Approval for a spectacular evening dress

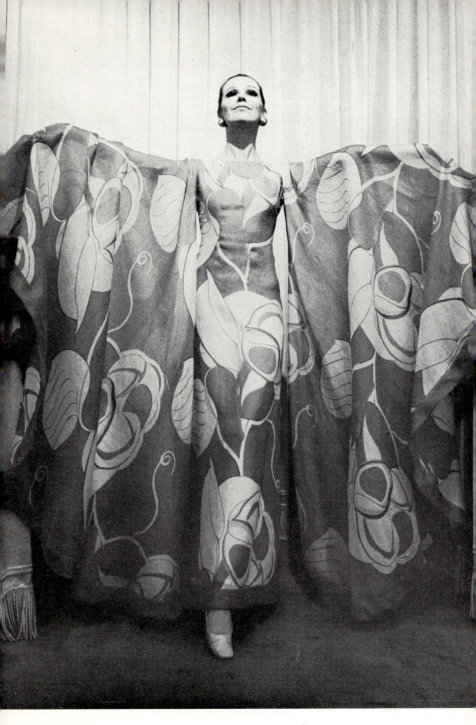

Haute Couture at its most dramatic

radiate. He also told me that the best models are American girls, when it comes to professionalism. English girls are usually debutantes filling in time until they get married, just looking for something to pass the time and not at all serious about their work, while in France the profession is only just becoming respectable. He said there was a fortune to be made by a girl with all the right attributes.

After some more shots in the studio, we jumped into his tiny Lotus sports car and buzzed around London while he took pictures of me standing on café tables, in the middle of the road, nearly being mown down by London taxis, and swinging around lamp posts. It was great fun, and I learned a lot of things about modelling that very first day, such as that if I ever wanted to work in the States I should have to lose fourteen pounds of the hundred-and-twenty-six which are distributed over my five foot nine inch frame, since they adore skeletons in New York, but for London I would probably make it as I was. As I had been trained as a dancer he told me that I had a natural sense of design in arranging my limbs in an interesting way, and that the best way to learn the business was to work with as many different photographers as possible for the experience.

In return for my day's work he gave me a set of pictures and a recommendation to the best agent in town, Peter Lumley. There are many other model agencies and many other models, as well as certain girls who describe themselves as models in order to lend glamour to a somewhat older profession. So I decided to begin right at the top. Before exposing myself to the critical expertise of Peter Lumley, I decided to become once more a natural blonde, and to have my hair cut in a really 'with it' style by the famous Vidal Sassoon. Usually I shunned hairdressers, and preferred to do my own with less mental anguish; but Vidal really understands where hair is at (people with disappearing hair please note), and of course he has a world-wide influence. His salon on Bond Street is a small but luxurious place, bursting at the seams with the most fabulous model girls and beautiful young men. Sitting next to me was Mary Quant, the *avant-garde* fashoin designer of 'swinging London'. Little did I know then that I would be showing her clothes one day quite soon. It was she who introduced the return of the 1920s look which has now lasted for almost a decade. Her part in the metamorphosis of staid old London into the 'swinging' city of today is indisputable. In fact if the Old Lady of Thread-needle Street were around nowadays, I am sure she would be leaping around in a mini-skirt, a see-through blouse and no bra!

The model girls that I noticed in Vidal's salon all seemed to have a certain look about them; a carefully-groomed disarray, a gauche elegance, a cultivated *au nature*, bordering on decadence, that was terribly attractive.

Vidal cut my hair beautifully. He made it short at the back and level with my chin in front, with a straight fringe down to my eyebrows so that I began to feel a little like Theda Bara. I felt quite different with it this way round and found it perfectly natural to slip into the droopy, helpless, rather gormless pose that was then all the rage.

Now, going for interviews scares me to death, and I take hours to get ready, changing my clothes about five times before I decide what to wear, checking and double checking in the mirror. But finally I made it to Peter Lumley's office and showed my photographs, which had turned out to be quite unlike what I had expected. I liked them, but best of all so did Peter Lumley, or Lumlugs as he is affectionately known. He decided to try me out. Naturally I told them I was an experienced model even though I had never even seen a fashion show let alone taken part in one. But you need a lot of *houtzpah* (a word I picked up in the rag trade, meaning cheek) in this business.

There are many schools where one can train to be a model and most of them have agencies for finding work for you on completion of the training. Some of these schools are genuine and only take girls who have earning potential, but many others put out advertisements in the papers stating that there is a fortune to be made and painting a glamorous picture of the profession, and are not sufficiently discriminating when they catch all kinds of innocent young and not so young girls, of all shapes and sizes who have no hope whatsoever of becoming models. They pay about forty guineas for this piece of optimism. But then perhaps a dream is worth any price.

My agency gave me a list of photographers, advertising agencies, and fashion houses, marked the photographers willing to work with beginners, and advised me to work at getting a book of photos together. I filled in a questionnaire giving my vital statistics, the colour of my hair, the state of my teeth, how many hair pieces I had, and details of my wardrobe and accessories. I of course had nothing except my genius for not taking things too seriously. They printed one of my photos in the *International Model Book*, which is a reference for casting, and rather like a stud book.

Some girls manage to combine photographic modelling with showing, and one of the first jobs I ever did was a fashion show in a stately home in Norfolk. It was a beautiful castle with a drawbridge and black swans sailing on the moat that surrounded it. Hounds were meeting there as we arrived, and the Master guffawed into his stirrup cup as we picked our way like giraffes from the cars, through a mass of wagging sterns and slobbering tongues and tweedy looking types. Dressing-rooms freezing cold, no heating, and the other models all experienced witches. They were able to pick out the best dresses and procure them for themselves. They knew a difficult dress on sight. Consequently I got the long red velvet sheath with heavy jewels round the hemline. It was a beast, and it felt just like walking with a ball and chain around one's ankles.

It just so happened that the catwalk was in a marquee in front of the castle on the lawn, and the dressing-rooms were in the east wing. In between there was a 100-yard passage ending at an impressively gigantic staircase, and then a further 50-yard dash through the Great Hall, over the drawbridge, and on to the catwalk. My very first catwalk. Quick changes were absolutely essential. The trick, I discovered while playing an elegant lady at Ascot in 4-inch heels and cartwheel hat before several hundred aged ogling admiring Conservatives, was to hurl off one's shoes, hitch up the dress to the waist, and to take the stairs two at a time. My prowess as a hurdler at school helped no end. It didn't take long for the press to discover where the real action was, and the photos that appeared of me the following day, all legs and arms and suspenders, were pretty sensational if nothing else. I also learned a lot about show modelling.

There are basically two types of modelling, and two types of model girls. There are those who do live fashion shows in a salon or on a runway or podium, and who are always impeccably dressed when you see them in the street en route for their many interviews, wearing full 'schlapp', or make-up all the time, including several pairs of false eyelashes. And then there are the photographic model girls. These very often look like nothing on earth in the flesh, slopping around in old clothes and no make-up, looking more like hippies than models; and yet when you see them in photos they look incredible. It's all in the bones. The facial structure is very important to photographers. Large features and tiny bones are essential. Hollow cheeks were the rage at this time, and some girls used to take a course of cheek-massage from a leading beautician to achieve this effect, whilst a few models even had their back teeth removed. Others alter their hairline with electrolysis to make a high forehead, like medieval noblewomen.

Then of course there is the eternal weight-losing game. I

know of one top photographic model who collapsed in the studio one day and was carried off to hospital. They discovered subsequently that she was suffering from malnutrition. Ever since Twiggy began setting the trend, this complaint has become increasingly common. So far I have never given a second thought to dieting. I ate like a horse and, being a dancer, worked it all off again. But my problems were to come when I went to Paris.

In spite of, or perhaps because of, the press sensationalism surrounding my debut at the Norfolk castle, I soon began to obtain more work. After a hard day's slogging from one studio to another with my heavy photographic book under my arm, I would arrive home and collapse, waiting for the agency to ring me with tomorrow's bookings. Fashion shows seemed harder to come by for the beginner.

It is fairly easy to spot a photographic model girl in the street when you see one. Apart from the occasionally hippie appearance, she is usually wearing a headscarf to cover up the enormous rollers in her hair, put in religiously between jobs, has on large black sunglasses to cover her eyelashes, and is dragging a huge bag around with her. This bag contains about five pairs of shoes, various scarves and accessories and hair pieces, and of course the book of photographs without which one could be arrested for not possessing an identity. Perhaps not arrested, but certainly frowned upon when image references are required.

After a few months I discovered that I was developing enormous biceps on my right arm. So I bought myself a large black leather bag with wheels on the bottom and the handles at just the right height for me when standing upright. It did make rather a noise especially over cobbles, but it was far less exhausting. Many is the time I wished I could have climbed into it and rolled off home. Of course a car was the answer, but apart from the terrible parking problem in London I never managed to save a penny. All my profits were ploughed back into the business, so to speak; that is to say, every available cent I earned went on clothes.

I shared a flat in World's End, Chelsea, with Barbara, a beautiful dancer with a passion for freaked-out hats. We used to wear each other's clothes. Sometimes we'd go for tea to Fortnum & Masons, and Barbara turned up one day wearing my black fox collar on her head, and a pair of Wellington boots, and looking as though she had just stepped from a Russian Troika instead of a number nine bus.

Before her marriage to a brilliant young film director, we were often invited for a Sunday morning pub crawl beginning at 'The Australian', a pub in Chelsea where lots of nice, young chaps from the 'in set' liked to appear at the weekend dressed in their St. Tropez gear. For a chap to become a member of 'the set' he needs either a title or a great deal of money, which he is prepared to spend on gambling, drinking, and parties. A girl needs for preference to be a model, with an additional rich daddy of some sort, so that she doesn't have to work too hard, and has the freedom to stay out until dawn at Anabelle's, and to take a little time off for Cowes week.

I adore sailing, not for any social reasons but simply because I love the sea and the wind. One night, at one of those 'I say what do you do', type parties, I was posed the standard question, by the usual rather harmless-looking chinless wonder. I replied, 'I'm a model'. 'How absolutely super', he answered. 'Would you like to come down to Cowes with me tomorrow?' I accepted, and we drove off the next day in his very smart Aston Martin.

When we arrived I had a surprise awaiting me. Instead of a beautiful yacht with a ten-man crew waiting to sail us anywhere we wished, there was a racy-looking speedboat, and my friend clambered into a black rubber suit and grabbed some water skis, asking me to drive the boat across to the Isle of Wight.

Now anyone who cares anything about sailing knows that the reaction of yachtsmen to speedboats is similar to that of Nelson upon first sighting the French fleet. Nevertheless I agreed to go along with this venture, hoping that we could putter into port quietly. But not a bit of it. Fifteen minutes later, we were sweeping into Cowes harbour at a reckless 50 m.p.h. past the Royal Yacht Britannia and then ZAP! We hit the shore with a thoroughly walloping crunch. The engine stalled and we drifted off, fouling the mooring lines of at least five other yachts with our tow rope, and then spent half an hour untangling things while the elders of the Royal Yacht Squadron watched us from the terrace and laced their gin-and-tonics with vitriol, and their Royal Majesties no doubt smiled in their gracious Britannic benevolence.

As we went ashore, a reporter from a gossip column snapped us, and inquired who we were. He was told 'Lord Fitzherbert and top model girl friend'. Gossip columns are insatiably impressed by such things. As for myself, the sheer absurdity of the situation had lent me a little distance – plus an equally absurd fit of the giggles. It was fun. Great calamitous fun.

But even so, Englishmen are best appreciated from a good distance. Ever since I went to live in Paris I have had nothing but nostalgia about them. But living amongst them in London was a different story. For instance I find that they normally have a puritanical suspicion of beautiful women. They assume that a beautiful woman must necessarily have a beautiful inflated ego, and that the best way to make contact with her is to put her down, thereby promoting themselves. Basically they adore women, but they are very definitely determined to keep them in their place, and consider this to be the best method. However, the more they pretend to ignore women, the more their domain is threatened. A chap I knew phoned me up one evening to invite me out, saying he would pick me up at 11.15 p.m. 'Why so late?' I enquired.

'The pubs don't close till 11', he replied openly. So he was going to spend the evening swilling pints of bitter with the other chaps and then come and breathe beer all over me! Hmm!

Lots of girls become dedicated beer drinkers themselves just so that they can be 'one of the boys'. Others become ardent Rugby or racing-car enthusiasts. And strange as it may seem, this brings me to my theory about the advent of mini-skirts.

There are various schools of thought on the origins of the mini-skirt. Some even say that it depends on the economy, i.e., the lower the economy the higher the skirts. Personally I think it was because women in England were sick and tired of being ignored and in a determined effort to be noticed at any cost decided to become sensational. Even so, walk down a street in London wearing something sensational, and British reserve and respect for the rights of an individual to do what she wants would still prevent any form of ogling. How to shock them into acceptance of women as a naturally desirable different species, that's the problem. If the average Englishman were to write his version of the Bible, 'Adam and Eve' would become the name of a favourite pub where it all started.

One day, the agency sent me to an interview with the house of Christian Dior in Conduit Street. The London branch of Dior is somewhat different from the Paris house, where of course everything is designed specially for the exclusive *haute couture* collection. London has its own designer, but the clothes aren't manufactured exclusively. They sell to stores as well as to private customers, while in Paris they make exclusively for private clients and for buyers from wholesale firms. Dior also sells men's clothes, ties and accessories. These are mostly manufactured in Bethnal Green, London, emblazoned with the magical name of the master, and subsequently sold for a small fortune. Even so, who can blame a house for 'going commercial' in this commercial age?

I was extremely nervous about the interview, but knew what a great prestige job it would be for me. They booked me, for very little money it's true, but it did great things for my status. Roger, my hairdresser, said, 'You can always tell when a girl is a success, she has that certain "air" about her'! I was so pleased and happy. The new route which my life had taken suddenly seemed to have been illuminated with signposts leading to a destination. I began to feel more comfortable with myself. It seemed to me that I had taken the turning off at the right moment, and that it had been a natural movement. That third person within myself, the one with the intense critical eye, was appeased.

The agency then rang and asked me to go down to Pinewood to see the casting director of a new film starring Peter Sellers. There was a part for a model, and with my theatrical and T.V. experience they thought I would be right for it. I was thrilled. This would be my big break I thought, on my way down to the studios. The casting director was charming. He looked me over and said that I had got the part. I had just to go home and wait by the telephone until they confirmed that same afternoon.

So I went home and stayed glued to the phone all day long. But do you know, that phone didn't ring once, and I finally gave up hope, and crept away, cursing miserably, to lick my wounds. The following day I discovered that the telephone was out of order. They had tried all afternoon to contact me and had finally given the part to someone else.

So I went straight up to the post office and threw a bomb through the window, smashed the switchboard with a sledge hammer and danced up and down on my hat, demanding one million dollars compensation for their part in the ruination of my career as a film star! At least, that's what I felt like doing. . . .

On my way home, for in fact I did go to the post office

and protest, I ran into an old friend. He happened to be just passing in his Rolls Royce, so I climbed in and unfolded my whole story to his sympathetic ears.

'Never mind darling'. He patted my shoulder. 'Come to a party at my place tonight and forget all about it. Peter will be there too'.

Kim Waterfield is a character well-known for giving the *chicest* parties in town. He's 'frightfully well-bred', rather languid, lives in a beautiful Georgian town house, has excellent taste and knows absolutely everyone. He is known as Dandy Kim to the gossip columnists. I loved his parties and he really is an excellent host. There was as always a great mound of caviar in the middle of a table laden with beautiful things, exquisite Baccarat glassware and Georgian silver. Sure enough, Peter Sellers was there, sitting shyly in a corner talking to himself with an intense 'don't come near me' look on his face.

At one stage a great booming theatrical row started up between Tom Courteney and Trevor Howard. Kim had a wonderful knack of stirring things up further for the entertainment of his guests, and hovered around like a referee at a prizefight throwing tiny spanners into the works. Finally a girl in a plaster cast from the top of her head down to her left ankle, who may even have been Dame Margot Fonteyn or the Invisible Man, broke it up by dancing a *pas de chat* on Courteney's foot with the plaster leg, and amid happy screams of agony the fête continued, as even more unlikely people arrived wearing beautifully improbable clothes, saying amusingly impossible things.

On Saturday morning in the King's Road Chelsea one may run into a few of the same people, each dressed to outdo the other and driving rare and obscure makes of cars. It costs a lot of money to keep up with this set; but not always. Some, seem to live on a budget that many a millionaire would find it hard to equal, and yet it's a well-known miracle that they haven't a cent.

Talking of millionaires, and I think I was, reminds me of a model with whom I became friends when we met during a fashion show in Cambridge. She had had nine abortions and was a little disillusioned with life, and suggested that the only way to happiness was through a rich man. Happiness was according to her, dollar-bill-shaped. I wouldn't say that she was hard exactly. She was just trying out the principle for size, and if she didn't like that one, well, she had others.

She introduced me to an American male whom she assured me was a perfect prospect for matrimony; i.e. aged sixty-five, incapable, and just slurping with oil wells. He phoned me a few days later with an invitation to dine at the Caprice, which I accepted being naturally fond of good food, and I rather liked him. I felt a little sad for him, being so lonely and so wealthy. Married three times, obviously to female predators. 'Am I one too?' I asked myself. The following day the gifts started arriving. First an enormous pink hydrangea, then a cashmere sweater, later on an expensive crocodile bag, and then a note asking me to call at Harrods and pick out some dresses. I never did get around to that one.

The following evening we went to Crockfords, the famous London gambling house. He went into a special room to play baccarat and gave me a five pound note to 'fool around with' at roulette. I had never gambled in my life or set foot inside a casino and even the sight of figures just makes my mind black out. However, I scattered the chips onto my favourite numbers, twenty-one, nineteen and seven, and didn't think about it too much. By the end of the evening I couldn't get those large square chips into my bag and even needed some help to carry them. I had made about £200.

It was around this time that the Inland Revenue were demanding two years of payment arrears. My winnings were just sufficient to take care of it. I don't know if the tax authorities would have approved or not, but I thought it was a novel way to appease my bureaucratic creditors.

When my American friend proposed marriage and suggested that I drive the Ferrari down to the Riviera to pick out a château for us to live in, asked what was my favourite fur and which jewels he should bring back for me from the States, and how would I like a nose job, I was perplexed. The 24-carat-gold-plated horns of a genuine chinchilla dilemma. I went through all the old clichés in my mind about 'not living in the clouds', being 'realistic', and 'not believing in fairies', and told myself to bear in mind the old style French marriage system – young girl marries old man, and then has streams of amorous lovers. More of a convenient alliance than true romantic love. I thought of my family, and how it would help them to have an infusion of gold into the exchequer, and then how we could afford a new roof for the house. I could buy my father that thirty-foot Bermuda sloop, and that horse for my sister and her family.

But I decided against the idea. Of course I like beautiful things, wealth and comfort and elegance; but it wasn't as important as all that and I thought that I could live without it whilst waiting for my fairy Prince Charming. The real one.

One day we went sightseeing to the Tower of London. There we came across three apple-pie American sailors aged about twenty. They were snapping pictures to send back home. They must have awakened some feeling of nostalgia in my American friend, he being a wartime ex-naval man himself, for he spoke to the three of them, inviting them back for a drink at his hotel. They were very respectful and were indeed extremely eager to accept the invitation. Then one of them said 'Excuse sir, but is this your daughter?'

I held my breath.

'No it's not!' he replied, with a tightly controlled benign aggressiveness. 'It's my sweetheart!'

I could have died, from a mixture of pity for my millionaire and a tinge of shame of myself; something which also helped to convince me that I had already made the right decision about my prospective mate.

Money! The fuel that stimulates the poor, and drives rich men to boredom. I certainly do not dislike money, though I'm a little afraid of the responsibility of possessions. But most of all, I suppose, I like the freedom that money can buy. I also have a sneaking suspicion that I would become horribly lazy if I had everything, and would cease to create anything. Necessity mothers all my inventiveness, so justly I need a struggle! Making one's fortune is much more fun than fun.

Most of the millionaires that I have met seem to be rather bewildered and lost, supported around the money belt by a retinue of sycophantic followers. It must be hard to sort out who your real friends are. Take Huntingdon Hartford for instance. He has more hangers-on than the last train out of Nagasaki. Well that's one problem I don't have.

If you really want to see the sights of swinging London, the Antique Supermarket is the place. Here you can buy all kinds of rare or common-or-garden junk, ranging from German coalscuttle helmets and iron crosses to spots for rocking horses. Also you may find there some real hundred per cent genuine London birds out shopping for their clothes. Owing perhaps to a kind of revolt against the consumer society, the second-hand clothing market is absolutely blooming. New clothes are out, and the 'in' dollies are far more excited by a long mauve dress, circa 1920, to wear with a feather boa, than by anything that Paris has to offer them. The 'fellers' wear ancient uniforms, ex-Hussars or Life Guards or even just plain old army surplus. Voluminous sleeves, lace ruffles and velvet are no longer considered 'pouffy' (or 'fag' if you prefer) and anyone with short hair is definitely out of place unless they happen to be female.

A friend of mine was given a droopy, pink-silk, cut-on-the-cross nightie, by a boyfriend who had found it in his mother's attic. She quite happily wore it all over town, along with a swansdown bedjacket. Divine!

Of course, to be an 'in bird', or 'feller', you also have to have the right accent. If your accent is Roedean or Oxford or 'How now brown cow', you can forget it. The accent most likely to succeed in London today is Stepney Green (Cockney). Every switched-on model girl and photographer develops a quaint old Dickensian yoi yoi! for business these days. You've got to be working-class to make it, even if Daddy was a Colonel out in Poona.

David Bailey is a good example of this. His career is something of a legend in the advertising world. It was he who 'made' Jean Shrimpton, or was it 'The Shrimp' who made David Bailey? Anyway they were never out of *Vogue* and *Harpers*; and David, looking very hippie and driving around in his Rolls Royce has made a fortune.

I first met the two of them when I was invited by Duffy, a well-known London photographer, to dinner at the Pickwick Club. Shrimp was incredibly beautiful, thin as a rake with lovely hollow cheeks and even taller than me. She brought her knitting and sat silently, clicking her needles all evening without a word. She was off to New York the following day. In the U.S. she was earning around 100 dollars an hour which compares rather favourably to the top London rate of around 15 guineas an hour. According to David Bailey, American photographers are the best in the world.

Photographers are a strange breed. Most of them appear to be over-sexed and cloak their basically lecherous instincts under the guise of art with a capital A. One I knew tried all sorts of ingenious methods to get me to strip off for a soap ad, in a bath, with steam and 'all terribly decent'. Some time later I discovered that he tried this one on every new model he came across — so I was glad that my shyness had stood me in good stead at last and ruined his ploy. Perhaps I sound like a prude, and in some ways I suppose I am. I don't like for example to do underwear ads, either. I would feel stupid having ten thousand people gazing at my navel in glorious technicolour on posters plastered all over the London Underground. (This seems to be the favourite art gallery for such optic happenings.) Although they do pay a lot of money.

I did once go for a job interview to a reputed bra and girdle manufacturer. They gave me a snow white girdle to put on, a bra, and a frilly pink lace peignoir over the top. Then they asked me to model it in front of five intense-looking business men. I walked up and down clutching the peignoir desperately. And after about five or six turns, they begged me to open it, but I just couldn't make it and fled from the salon like a woodland nymph surprised by satyrs.

Somehow I find that complete nudity is much less offensive than the 'semi' kind of bras and girdles. It must be a question of aesthetics. However, thank God, the days of the girdle are numbered and we can now wear tights instead of ugly suspenders or the even more hideous garter belts. I don't care if some men do find them sexy.

Another photographer I know delights in shocking his victims, especially if they are young innocents fresh from school. His conversation is mined like a battlefield with four-letter words. He'll get you lined up for a shot and then just as he's about to take it he'll casually enquire about some intimate aspect of the animal side of one's nature, but in an extremely crude fashion. Then as your eyes open in surprise and your lower lip trembles with shock, he will take the picture, achieving some quite remarkable effects. But then he is also extremely talented and he does take fabulous fashion photos and is very successful, so perhaps the end does justify the means.

There is no doubt about the fact that an awful lot of charming young men who hardly know one end of a camera from another set themselves up as being photographers solely as a way of meeting streams of beautiful 'chicks' and being part of the swinging scene. Since Princess Margaret married a photographer the profession has become a very 'in' thing.

Norman Parkinson is a very serious artist and tremendous fun to work with. He looks rather like an English army major, with a bristling waxed moustache. He wears a little jewelled skull cap when he's working, and laughs a lot and plays groovy music to relax you. But sometimes it is difficult to relax, as when you're dangling over the Thames in a painter's cradle suspended from a scaffold, wearing a thin summer dress in sub-zero temperature, and the photographer says 'O.K. Smile'.

T.V. commercials are a great source of income and sometimes fun to do. Once I was chosen to do an ad for Terylene. The location was Monkey Island on the river Thames. In order to demonstrate the miraculous advantages of the materials I was wearing (a pink pleated skirt and frilly white blouse), I was expected to punt a boat up river, get stuck on the punt pole and end up in the water whilst the straw boater I was wearing floated off down stream. It took about one month to shoot the thing due mainly to the machinations of the English summer. I was paid vast sums of money whilst I gazed, not too gloomily, at the rain.

Between takes, I had a chance to reflect a little on my career. I came to the conclusion that in order really to make it as a top photographic model, you need either (a) a photographer to fall madly in love with you, (b) your back teeth removed and maybe your frontal brain lobes, and/or (c) to fall madly in love with yourself. The latter is maybe indispensable in any case. Not sour grapes – merely the vintage wine that a little maturity brings.

Reluctantly, I felt unable to comply with any of these conditions, so I decided to concentrate upon fashion shows Such shows appeal to the exhibitionist in my nature. I love to strut around and be stared at. I am a show off. Also the designers and the men who arrange fashion shows, the rag trade Ziegfields, adore women but usually on pedestals and from afar. It is a question of pure aesthetics, or almost pure anyway. So one is never bothered with the old clichés, 'I can get you on the front cover of *Vogue*, give you a leading part in my next film, show you the casbah etc., etc.'

Suddenly the lightning struck. 'I'll go to Paris!' I said to myself. 'There I shall become a legend', and I thought of Coco Chanel and Isadora Duncan, and decided there and then that Paris being the indisputable centre of the *haute couture* industry, that's where I should be, irrespective of the old adages about selling refrigerators to the Eskimos or exporting whisky to Scotland.

There was however a snag. I hadn't saved a single cent (though I had lots and lots of shoes), there was no millionaire in sight, and the credit squeeze had successfully frozen the smile upon the bank manager's face. I decided to do a season in London. That is, to work for six weeks in a wholesale fashion house, showing twice a day to buyers from all over the country at a fee of ten guineas per day, and to save as much of it as I could. The money that I was earning whilst having these thoughts would serve as a useful launching pad.

Some of these vacant stares that one sees upon the faces of people between takes on a film set are not quite so innocuous as they look.

It was on my first day working for Roter models that I met Felicity. She was fixing her hair and hogging the only mirror (she was always fixing her hair) when I turned up on Monday morning. She was very tall and slim, with beautiful thick dark hair piled on top of her head and large slanting dark eyes. Her face had a sophisticated, sultry look about it which was completely at variance with her nature. For, with the exception of her dark hair, Felicity was the original 'Lauralie'. She was completely childlike, with the attention span of a gnat and the memory of a sieve, together with some kind of primordial wisdom which looked after her welfare. But she was so funny and so full of *gentillesse*, that no one could fail to adore her. When she wasn't modelling she used to go home to Margate and help with the potato digging on one of the local farms, for relaxation. She was an outdoor type. One day she bought a pot of lotion that tans you without the sun, and proceeded to cover herself in it from head to toe. Four hours later she had turned a delightful dark yellow, with patches of pink on her forehead and legs, and appeared to have an insipient moustache. Mr. Roter was a dear. He took one look at her when she appeared in the showroom and then muttered to his wife that he would really have to do something about the lighting.

The clothes at Roter Models all looked rather Hollywood 1950, and the boss would not permit anything but stiletto heels and pointed toes and hated the new styles. But they were very kind people to work for, despite their 'play it safe' fashions. Besides, they were making money, lots of it, and business is business is business!

One day Felicity decided that she wanted long elegant fingernails (her own were bitten unmercifully), and she bought a kit of stick-on false nails. She passed the entire day sticking them on, and was even late leaving work at the end of the day. We had a date for drinks that evening with two boys from ad agencies. Thus there we were, elegantly ensconced on the plush seat of a cocktail bar, when Felicity reached out five prehensile talons in order to scratch her head, in spite of my subtle signals to her. When she brought her hand down again, the nails stayed where they were, clinging to her chignon and looking rather like hard confetti. We retired to the ladies room shaking with silent hysterical laughter.

I told Felicity of my plan to go to Paris in June, and she was awestruck by the idea. She had never been abroad before.

'Oh Val, I wish I could do something like that', she breathed.

'You can', I replied, 'if you want to. Why not?'

Felicity however also had a few money problems which we had to solve before we could take off together (literally), and thus it was that we got into Felicity's bathing beauty scheme. She had heard that a local 'whisky à go-go' club was holding a beauty contest, and she decided to enter in it as a means of building a financial cushion for our ultimate landing. First she borrowed a bikini of mine, a leftover from a cover-girl shot I once did for the *Daily Mirror*, and we proceeded to stitch her into it. Now Felicity, for all her sophisticated, sultry elegance, wasn't just tall — she was powerful . . . and yet she had a pink-check-gingham personality. After we had managed to shoe-horn her into the garment, what there was of it, we perfumed and powdered her and stood back from the mirror to appraise our chances. We both agreed that they looked pretty good; and covering her with a large drape — we took a taxi to the club.

Talk about the fat stock sales! We were shown into a cramped changing-room where about thirty beauty queens were being 'rubbed down' by their mothers. Some mothers were busy coating their offspring with tanning lotion, some were sewing last-minute sequins onto appropriate places and others were building up bouffant blonde hairdos to dizzy heights and then spraying the effigy with hair lacquer. None of the girls spoke to each other if they could possibly help it, and communication was through the language of the eyes, sidelong glances of unutterable loathing and, if the opportunity arose, perhaps a little mocking pity. Such was the reaction to one obvious novice to 'the business' who had neglected to paint herself chocolate brown, and whose flesh appeared by contrast to be a delicate and most unsexy duck-egg blue! The seasoned, I noticed, had spurned the conventional bikini and preferred to wear pull-in, push-up, squeeze-out bras and panties, covered with ersatz leopard skin or gold lurex.

There was about the whole scene an air of primitive ritual, as of preparation for some ancient fertility rite. I could hear the sound of what might have been warriors doing a war dance, coming from the club. Presently I went and stood out there to watch the contest, having first assured Felicity of my undying support. The warriors turned out to be mostly pint-sized yobos from Golders Green, and they cleared the floor at a given command from the 'big chief yobo' with the microphone, forming a semi-circle around a pool of light.

One by one the girls teetered in on their six-inch heels, amidst a chorus of bird noises, howls, and primordial cries. Each one appeared to me to have short thighs, tall hair, and a glassy grin. Felicity was about ninth on the list. Now the ceiling at the 'whisky à go-go' was rather low, which only accentuated the fact that every one there seemed to have come straight out of *Gulliver's Travels*. It also accentuated Felicity's legs as they came on and on, and on, and on . . . and as the spotlight travelled up, and up, and up, and the human aviary sounds reached a Bacchanalian crescendo of appreciation. Felicity was indisputably the out-and-out winner. In fact it was a classic case of the old show biz 'Follow that!'

We went home that night with terrific lightness of heart, and £100 the heavier in the purse.

4

FIRST DAYS IN PARIS

The night tourist-flight to Paris left at midnight. I was alone as I stepped on board. Felicity had gone on ahead and we had a rendezvous in the Champs Elysées for the following day. It must have been around 2 a.m. when I arrived in Paris. I took a taxi to the Rue du Civry in the 16th arrondissement where a friend had lent me his Paris pied à terre; the key was to be left under the mat for me. I paid off the taxi, lugged my three heavy suitcases up the steps and into the elevator, out of the elevator, and of course – no key! Hot, sweating, what do I do now? Find hotel. Drag cases down again. Pitch dark. Not a soul. No taxis. Eventually I find one and explain the predicament as best I can. No French money either. He agrees to accept a pound note.

'Hotel – anywhere!' I don't know Paris at all. I try to explain to him in my pidgin French, '*Je ne connais pas Paris de tout*'. Trust him. '*Arc de Triomphe*?' I added. It was all I could think of apart from '*sous les ponts*'.

'O.K. meeze'.

I was hot, tired and miserable, and felt a long way from home. Did I really want to be a cosmopolitan after all? We stopped at a small hotel somewhere, and I knocked at the door. An upstairs window shot open and Dickens' 'Madame Defarge' looked out, croaked something obscene, and went back to her knitting.

The next hotel was brighter and the door was open

invitingly. There were two women of about thirty-five at the desk. One of the two was rather heavily made-up, and their eyes were full of pins and needles.

'Are you a major?' one asked me.

'Just a lance-corporal', I sighed; but the 3 a.m. humour seemed to escape her.

'Are you over twenty-one?' she snapped.

'*Mais oui*'.

'Then there will be a room free in half an hour', she said.

The time was by then, in fact precisely, 3.15 a.m. 'What a strange time to check out', I innocently thought and went to explain this to my taxi driver, who laughed, apologised and took me to yet another place where I finally found a bed at last.

I climbed between the sheets and dreamed that I was walking down an *Haute Couture* runway, showing a beautiful green check suit, with a high collar and cuffs of chinchilla. At the foot of the runway I turned and unbuttoning the jacket slipped it off elegantly, to show the blouse. But in true Freudian nightmare style, I was stark naked underneath! The crowd roared. I was rooted to the spot, and when I tried to run away, my legs became like spaghetti in slow motion. And then I awoke. . .,.

It had been one of these dreams which make reality much more bearable by comparison, so I felt quite optimistic when the following morning I set about constructing my disorder into a recognisable chaos. There had been a mix-up about my arrival date, I discovered when I contacted my friend Charles about the apartment, and consequently the key would be under the mat tonight instead. Thus encouraged I checked out of the hotel. Taking my optimism in both hands I went to meet Felicity at the *Café Pergola*, in order that we could discuss our plan of campaign.

Naturally she was not there. The appointed hour came and went, and the beer began to resemble the flattened state of my hopes. Even so, it became suddenly wonderful fun. Being in Paris. The sheer extravagant escapade of it. That pale golden sun that one sees in Paris. Chic women as they passed. The *clochards* making faces at me through the window of the pavement café, begging for my elusive fortune. Elusive to me that was; to them I was Lady Bread and Butter.

Now I have never been known for my punctuality either, but Felicity really takes the prize. So at intermittent intervals I cursed to myself as I waited, imagining her fiddling with her false nails or eyelashes or hair. When finally she arrived all flustered and apologetic, it turned out that she had got hopelessly lost on the *Metro* and some kind gentleman had offered his 'help' and she had, according to Felicity, all but found herself shipped off on a boat to Morocco as part of the white slave trade. I was suitably horrified. By then it was too late to do anything about jobs, so we relaxed and just took in the scene.

The following day, we ended up on a *Bateau Mouche* with three charming Americans whom we had met outside the Louvre. Somehow it's difficult to be snooty to your fellow travellers when you are all brought together by a common affliction; that is, suddenly you have all become foreigners! In spite of the great number of years that I had spent trying to learn French from a Welshman, I was not far beyond a few verb conjugations and a couple of derogatory French songs. Felicity knew nothing but 'Oh la la!' So we were hardly equipped for the literary set. Fortunately most French people speak English, especially in the *couture* business.

We had given ourselves a week to find work and that allotted time was rapidly slipping through our fingers and what we had spent in a week would probably have lasted a whole month in England. However this is one of the hazards of this city that one has to come to terms with, if you want to enjoy living here. All the same, we couldn't afford to lose time.

Nevertheless, it was already Thursday before we finally made our assault on the bastions of the high priests of *couture*, with the aid of a lot of bravado and two pairs of false eyelashes each. Our plotting and planning paid off, and irrespective of the near realisation of my hotel dream, which Balmain brought vividly to life with his hilarious reception of my *haute couture* model act, we were in, accepted – and in fact even welcomed. It was a triumph of feminine, scatter-brained, allergy to reason. 'We make our own destiny' goes the saying of the prophet, and to a large extent I have discovered it to be a true cliché. Perhaps it is the sauce provided by the exceptions that really gingers up the mixture.

I learned that Balmain likes to begin fittings at the beginning of July; this being two weeks or so away I had some time to embroider. Felicity had to start work immediately at Lanvin, so I left her in Paris while I returned to England to collect more clothes, clear up my affairs, and to tell the joyful and improbable news to my agents. They were thrilled, and immediately I found all kinds of newspapermen on my doorstep. I found myself suddenly faced with pressing demands for interviews and candid newspaper photographs. Apparently the last English girl to work for Balmain had been Bronwen Pugh, who while showing the collection at St. Moritz had met her future husband. (He saw her on the podium and fell in love with her at first sight.) She subsequently became Viscountess Astor – one of the wealthiest families in Europe – and since then she had hardly been out of the gossip columns. I began to feel like a star.

All my family were thrilled by the news too, and when I walked up our village street with my mother she simply had to stop and tell everyone that her daughter was now a Paris model. I nearly died of embarrassment, but then mothers are like that, *n'est ce pas*? The landlord of our local pub, where we all went to celebrate, was pleased too, though he couldn't

quite understand why I should choose to go to such a
barbaric place as Paris. A lot of Englishmen still keep the
old-fashioned colonial prejudice that 'wogs begin at Calais!'
and he agreed with them. 'But I'll tell Spider to look after
you', he promised. Spider is the ghost of an old hunting
groom who got bricked up in the chimney by mistake many
years ago, and has haunted the ancient 15th century inn ever
since. It was a magnificent family send-off, and the following
day I took off again for Paris.

Somebody once remarked on what great 'pick-up' places
aeroplanes are, since one meets such interesting people. It is
true, I suppose. I've noticed the way that seasoned male
travellers, especially Americans, size up the talent in the
departure lounge and very often jockey for position when
they see a good-looking girl, elbowing each other out of the
way as they angle for the seat next to hers. I know some girls
who even go so far as to make a point of getting themselves
chatted up by someone during the flight, just so that they
may have a little help with their bags, and maybe also free
lifts into town.

From time to time I have in fact met interesting people on
the London to Paris flight. I once found myself sitting next
to a world famous racing driver. He was on his way to
compete in the European Grand Prix and sat with a crash
helmet in his lap discussing crankshafts and overdrives and
sprocketts with a team-mate. It wasn't too difficult to guess
his profession; besides I had seen his picture in a newspaper.
Perhaps he had also seen mine for that matter. We got
chatting, and he being a Scot and I being a direct descendant
from the ancient Highland clan chief Cumin (family motto
'Sans Peur'), we found that we had a lot in common. Upon
arrival, I would have had to go through all the trouble of
getting my bags to the airport bus, then from bus to taxi, had
it not been for the fabulous Masserati, which my travelling
companion had waiting for him.

Felicity had moved into a hotel, together with a South African model girl called Henrietta whom she had met on her first day at Lanvin, and they had arranged for me to stay there too. It was a hot sultry summer night as my fast moving Scot and I drove around searching for my hotel — it turned out to be right in the heart of Irma la Douce country, 'Les Halles'. Not the most salubrious of neighbourhoods! Hen and Fifi, as they were subsequently called, were sitting outside the downstairs café as we drove up, and after all the reunions and introductions were over I said goodbye to my charming knight errant and we all three went into the crumbling hotel.

The room I was to share with Fifi was stifling. It was on the fifth floor with a spiral stairway leading up to it. 'Quaint', and 'typical', and 'bags of character' are some of the words Henrietta used to describe it. I suppose the large creaky iron bedstead was rather quaint, and the dark grey lace curtains, you might say were typical, and you could also say that the whole feeling that it gave one, principally that of having stepped into a seedy old French film starring Jean Gabin, was indeed reeking with character.

Henrietta's room was on the first floor. There were no telephones in the rooms, which was not really of importance for in order to converse from room to room one merely had to raise one's voice a semitone, it was then amplified to a grandiose magnitude in the well which rose up from the courtyard down below. It was a kind of whispering gallery.

Above one of the beds in our room was a notice which said, *'Defense de pousser les crie de joie'*. That did not seem to deter any of the other residents however, and a sleepless night was had by all.

The following day we decided to look for an apartment together. So I bought a *Herald Tribune* and we found a three-room apartment in St. Germain des Prés advertised for 750 francs a month. When we went along to see the place, we all three fell in love with it on the spot. It didn't seem to matter that one of the rooms was also the bathroom, that one of us would have to sleep on the floor on a mattress, that the furniture appeared to have come from a local park, and that all this was a 6th floor walk-up! The angles of the roof, the ancient beams and the tiny balcony draped in flowers, and the fact that it was right in the heart of the Latin Quarter, made up our minds for us. Besides, the attic was that same original attic where Victor Hugo had starved as he wrote his classic *Les Miserables*.

The learned left-bank lady who owned it was leaving for Ibiza for the summer. We took it and moved in almost immediately. And so began three blissful months of getting to know each other, putting up with each other, and finally learning to live with each other. We were all three very different characters. Felicity (or Fifi) you know already. Henrietta was exactly her opposite. I like to think that I provided some kind of communicative link between them. Henrietta was a perfectly splendid organiser, especially of herself. She was engaged, and was to be married quite soon to an Englishman and though she was South African she was more British than the British themselves, if you know what I mean. I sometimes used to hear her lecturing Fifi, saying, 'When you are abroad you are an ambassador for your own country, and you must never let the side down'. You'd think she was going on Safari to the Belgian Congo, judging by the quantity of provisions and medical supplies which she had brought with her from England. Boxes and boxes of Tampax and Kleenex and tea and English marmalade. Enough to relieve the seige of Mafeking.

Henrietta was having a last fling before settling down to married life and babies. She was also the only one of us capable of being sensible about money. She was saving up. So whilst Fifi and I got through most of our salary in one week by flitting around in taxis, and then remained broke for the rest of the month or took an advance, Henrietta managed on ten francs a day and even saved some of that!

We spent the weekend installing ourselves in the apartment, and after drawing lots, Fifi had the bedroom, Hen got the bed in the bathroom, and I slept on the mattress under the skylight and felt just like *La Bohême*!

Monday morning was my first day at Balmain, and it was quite a scene as all three of us fought for the bath, and the only mirror, and endeavoured to fix eyelashes on to half-awake lids and climb into girdles and remember where we had just put things, and not to let the coffee boil over and to keep smiling throughout.

Eventually we all three clattered down the stairs and out into the delicious morning sunshine of the Rue du Dragon, and parted company, Hen and Fifi going to the Metro and myself to the taxi rank. Start as you mean to go on in life, is my credo. . . .

5

C'EST CA LA HAUTE COUTURE!

That legendary institution *la haute couture*, that glossy, freaky, high tension world of superlatives, extravaganza, froth, frills and frivolity where the extraordinary becomes ordinary and the way out becomes the way in, is deep down *au fond*, a world of big business involving millions of dollars. It abounds in paradoxes. Where they think nothing of investing thousands in a full-length evening dress of white ermine, they will quibble over the price of a button, and whilst the entire collection, complete with mannequins, might be flown to Bangkok for a special showing for the Queen of Thailand, they will think twice about paying extra to a mannequin who has posed for a series of photos of the collection. It seems that even in the *haute couture* business, businesss is business.

This sordid hard core of commerce and business however does not directly affect the mannequins. Living in the world of *haute couture* is just a little like living up on a Xmas Tree; all sweetness and tinkley light, where the mannequins are the adornments on the tree and vie incessantly with one another for the position as fairy upon the top. They must be found strange or beautiful enough to inspire the designer to create, and also to inspire the customer to buy the creation. For this latter service we receive the honorary sum of one franc commission per dress. Not exactly a fortune, but worth its weight in ego-fodder. On those very rare occasions, for this is *haute couture*, that a mannequin actually inspires the sale of 100 dresses, it is her golden opportunity to buy a bottle of the very best champagne for a general celebration in the *cabine*. In any case it simply isn't at all true that most mannequins are gold-diggers. The majority would far rather show something outrageously beautiful which gets a round of applause, than that safe little number which is likely to sell. (Not that 100 dresses at one franc a time, less a bottle of the best champagne, would be likely to launch us on Wall Street.) Anyway, speaking as a self-confessed narcissist, who sees no harm in indulging her complex now and then, I love admiration and I think this goes for all mannequins. Whether the admiration is in reality for the dress, the designer, or for something quite different is of little or no consequence, in so far as the mannesquin is concerned that dress has become a part of her, she is expressing it, and she revels in the applause. I do at least. Perhaps I still have more than a little of my earlier show biz experience in my veins, but I think it helps to be able to give oneself to a dress.

Preparations for the collection have been going on for several weeks before the *pose* actually begins, with such vital things as selecting materials and trimmings. Representatives from exclusive and famous textile houses and button manufacturers and many others come round during this time to present their latest wares, and samples of embroidery, belts and buttons being pinned to the wall. Balmain chooses about 300 different samples of cloth, gorgeous silks and prints and chiffons if it is the summer, and wools and tweeds if it is for the winter collection. The spring collection is shown at the end of January, and perversely the winter collection is shown in July (usually during a heat-wave). Probably Balmain will use only about half the materials he has invested in.

Every collection costs about 300,000 dollars to put on and there are around 100 to 150 garments shown. Prices range from 600 dollars for a suit to around 3,000 dollars for an evening dress. And this does not mean alas, that the poor little rich girls will have bought the only one in existence, for a successful number, may sell fifty or sixty times from the *couture* house, quite apart from the manufacturers' copies. You can of course buy the model exclusively if you are really insistent — for an extra 6,000 dollars!

The *cabine* at Balmain can become like the black hole of Calcutta, but at the beginning of the *pose* it is absolutely bare. Nothing remains of the previous collection, and the rows of empty rails are just waiting for the new creations to arrive. At one end of the room is a long dressing table, the mirror with lights round it, and in front of each separate place there is a chair with a name emblazoned across the back, just like a film star's. This is not altogether inappropriate, as I discovered that *les mannequins* as we are called in Paris, are pampered and spoilt in exactly the same fashion. We are, after all, expected to be part-actress (as I tell myself), changing mood according to the mode of the dress, lending it that touch of drama, romanticism, gaiety, or sophistication. Once during the final rehearsals for the collection I was showing an enormous red fox fur coat. The furs went round and round, not up and down, it was one of those coats for burrowing deep down inside. On my head I wore a black jersey helmet that came down over my eyebrows and ears with a scarf covering the chin. I was wearing the palest of make-up, the reddest of lips, and the blackest, thickest and longest lashes that I could find. I flashed onto the podium with all the arrogance of a Spanish dancer; then I heard Balmain exclaim, 'Wonderful. Lady Bread and Butter looks so hard and bitchy like that!'

I'm sure that if any of my men friends came across me in that state they would run a mile, but for the couture one is permitted to act like a prima donna, both on and off the podium. In fact the more tantrums you throw, the more spoilt you appear, the more demanding, unreasonable, extravagant, eccentric, not to say cranky that you appear, the better they love you, just so long as you turn up for work on time and have, above all, the charm to get away with it all!

But of course I was just a new girl and as yet unaware of these freaky behavioural patterns.

In the *cabine* there are *les habilleuses* or dressers, and each has a stable of two mannequins. They have all been with the firm for years, and may live in extreme poverty themselves whilst sharing in the brilliant, glamorous, highly-scented world of their mannequins. They are like possessive mother-hens with their charges, and share in all their glories as well as the intimate secrets of their private lives. They are given clothes by Balmain from time to time. My dresser's name is Edith; she comes from *le Midi*, as the French call the South of France, and she has the typical accent of the region. It took me two years really to learn to follow what she was saying, since she speaks so quickly. She is married to a *gendarme* and has been with the firm for fifteen years. She is tremendously quick and efficient as well as being an adorable person. Strangely enough the *habilleuses* are the only people who are ever able to bully the mannequins; and sometimes it takes quite a bit of bullying to pour nearly six feet of languid girl into tights, blouse, suit, boots, hat, gloves and earrings, zip her up, and push her through the curtains on time. If she doesn't make it, it is the *habilleuse* who gets the blame and never the mannequin, as everybody knows that a mannequin is a long, droopy pea-brained creature, incapable of coherent thought and merely a being, an exotic thing, madly in love with her own reflection!

After a few days of getting to know the *cabine*, saying little and observing a lot, the buzzer went on the desk of the dragon-like *chef de cabine* and I first heard the dreaded cry that was to become so familiar, '*Valerie! Au Studio vite!*' I hastily grabbed one of the white overalls which we are all

Even models sometimes travel by bus

A break for lunch at 'La Belle Ferronierre'

given to cover our bras and girdles during the *pose* and shot off up the stairs, to the hot, busy room, where there are no windows and no sound but the hum of the air conditioner, plus an occasional scream as someone gets stuck with a pin. This is the studio, which adjoins the inner sanctum wherein sits *le patron* flanked by Eric Mortensen and his other worthy accomplice Monsieur Raymond from Pekin, to add just a further touch of exoticism to the scene.

Eric is Balmain's right arm. They have worked together for a number of years and Balmain uses him as a sounding-board upon which to sharpen his creative wits. The combination of clear-cut Scandinavian simplicity with Latin appreciation of fine detail and subtlety seems to spark off inspiration after inspiration. Apart from Eric's amazingly boyish good looks, and his unique capacity for the icy 'put down', he also possesses a great sense of humour and has an endless fund of tales to tell about past mannequins. He's seen them all come and go. Raymond runs around being inscrutable and lending an oriental flavour to the general ambience.

There were three spider-legged fitters in the studio that first day, each spinning a *toile* over a victim. The *toile* is the pattern of the dress, which is cut out in rough calico and fitted on to the mannequin before being cut in the final material. I hovered around and took in the scene for an instant. Just then the patron came through and saw me standing there.

'Bonjour cherie, comment allez vous?' he said exuberantly. Summoning up my fractured French, 'Tres bien', I replied 'et toi?'

There was a pregnant hush in the studio and people exchanged shocked glances. Then the patron began to chuckle, and then just simply roared with laughter. I had no idea why, and wondered what on earth I could have done this time. Everyone was giggling by then. When the laughter had finally subsided, I learnt that in France it is very familiar to use *tu* instead of *vous* and you certainly never *tutoyer* the patron. (French humour. I wonder if Louis XVI really found it so funny just prior to Robespierre, or whoever it was, cutting off his head.)

Balmain adored my *faux pas* though, and every morning after that we used to go through the same routine just for fun.

Since our first dramatic meeting during my audition, I have discovered that Balmain laughs a lot. He is extremely extrovert and demonstrative, and adores to dance and to sing. He has a vast repertoire of obscure traditional French songs (some of them anti-British) which he will sail into, grabbing hold of you and waltzing you around the salon with joy. He loves his work, and his mood reflects the state of the creation, and in its turn the mood of the whole establishment is likewise a reflection of himself. If for instance the *pose* is slow and Balmain has not yet been inspired, then everyone is miserable, and the fitters creep around talking in subdued whispers. Monsieur Eric and Raymond look straight through you as though you were made of glass, and all the mannequins begin to feel unloved and persecuted as if it were all their fault. But once he has found the line then the word goes round and the world starts spinning again. You can hear him singing as he works, and everyone starts to love each other once more.

Balmain came, originally, from the *Haute Savoie*, and quite often employs people from this area. His early life was spent training for architecture, in which he is still passionately interested, and which must have had a strong influence over his *couture* designs — quiet, elegant simplicity, exquisitely cut, is the hall-mark of a Balmain creation.

Naturally, in such a highly competitive and capricious business as the *haute couture*, where ones livelihood and that of an entire concern, comprising about 600 employees, depends upon the mystical and sometimes inexplicable fashion trends, and occasionally the whims of wealthy women, it is somewhat difficult for a couturier to be on friendly terms with his closest rivals. Pierre Balmain indeed provides no exception to this rule. He has fought long and hard for his lonely perch at the top of the tree. When so much depends on publicity and *snobbism*, it is important for a couturier to mingle in the right kind of high society and thus to attract well-known women and titles to his salon. With his impeccable English and witty extrovert humour, Balmain is thus well known socially and frequently gives very select and elegant parties at his gorgeous mansion at Croissy on the Banks of the Seine, just on the outskirts of Paris. I have sometimes attended these parties and they are wonderful affairs, rather like something from the middle ages in their pomp and splendour. Sometimes he will in turn attend some very chic jet-set ball at Versailles, or a gala night at Deauville along with *le tout Paris*, and I have heard him describing in detail to Eric exactly who was there, what they were wearing, plus (most important) by whom they were dressed.

Another occasion that very often helps the business along is, surprisingly enough, when a new state becomes independant. When this happens, as Balmain says, 'There is a whole new race of officials' wives who must have "Something from Paris" '. The guest-list at the special V.I.P. preview of his collection reads like a selection from *Debrett's Peerage* or *Who's Who*. Balmain, with his quiet good taste, his care for the aesthetics, and his fine eye for beauty, does not exactly supply sensation *couture*, but his worth is well demonstrated by the number of extremely wealthy customers who come to him.

Often in the *couture* business I have heard a *vendeuse* refer to somebody whom I have considered to be extremely chic and well-dressed. *'Oui, mais elle ne fait pas l'haute couture!'* For a long time the subtleties escaped me. Now, having been dressed exclusively by Balmain for a number of years, I too, can spot the difference. It would be a major catastrophe if

one turned up wearing a lace blouse with a check suit, or a
handbag that was too small or too large for the outfit, or the
wrong earrings or, major sin! a hemline not of the stipulated
length. The list of crimes against *la mode pure* is endless, and
contravention of any of them could cause a *vendeuse* to
make deep French clucking noises in her throat and refuse to
speak to you until you had recovered your senses. I once
overheard two fitters discussing a seam as though it was a
work of the most sublime art, admiring the cut and the
intricate hand-stitching whilst exclaiming breathlessly, 'Voila!
C'est ca l'haute couture!'

It does give one a tremendous feeling of confidence to know
that one is wearing something exquisite. Besides, Frenchmen
invariably notice and recognise a beautiful clothes *ensemble*
too. From taxi drivers to barons, they are all absolutely
fascinated by *la mode*. To the average Frenchman, being well
dressed is just as important a part of living as good food;
unlike the average Englishman who, as I mentioned earlier,
would lover his eyes and smile politely if you turned up in
your birthday suit. I've even known complete strangers in
France to cross the street in a purposeful manner merely to
tell me that my skirt is too short, or too long, or that they
appreciate my crazy stockings. In this way I have very often
been confronted with a demand to know who my couturier is.

I was once standing on the *Metro*, clinging with one hand
to the pole in the middle, wearing a red-and-white coat with
wine-coloured gloves, hand-bag and shoes. A studious-looking
gentleman reading *Le Monde* and clinging to the other half of
the pole suddenly folded up his newspaper, fumbled in his
top pocket, gravely produced a pair of scissors, and proceeded to snip off a threat hanging off one of my gloves.
Then he calmly put the scissors away again muttering, 'Tch,
Tch, it's a pity to spoil a beautiful outfit!', and returned to
his newspaper.

At a chic Parisian party, a girl will frequently be pointed

out as 'that beautiful girl wearing the Dior'. Just as the Frenchman's palate has been developed to appreciate the most subtle and exquisite nuances in *la haute cuisine*, so his eye is alert for dress and beautiful women; '*la haute couture* been extended to a fine point of aestheticism. In spite of all this however, in its present form it is a beautiful dying art. More and more couturiers are going over to mass production, usually for economic reasons. I suppose there are no longer enough queens and duchesses to go round, and nowadays almost anyone can dress like a duchess at a fraction of *couture* prices. A quiet revolution is taking place at the moment. A revolution that could lead the *haute couture* business to a beautiful, unfashionable, funeral. People are revolting against the accepted standards of good taste and beauty, and against the uniformity that the consumer age has brought about. Therefore they are no longer willing to accept the dictates of fashion designers, but prefer to dress according to their own feeling. The young people are wearing exactly what they like. Anything goes. No longer is it considered necessary to suffer chapped knees in winter through being a slave to fashion, or to feel obliged to wear ones skirt at mini length irrespective of ones own good sense. In winter we shall wear maxi skirts and in summer mini skirts. What could be simpler.

This transition period of blasting down the barriers of conformity will last for a while until eventually a new stability evolves, with new standards; and eventually the cream will rise to the top, the best will come into its own and we shall then have a new *haute couture*. One that really deals with seasonal and temperamental aesthetics, perhaps. The variations, and occasional mischief, of nature's climate will then be a blessing for the fashion-conscious woman rather than an alien effect to be tolerated, for we shall no longer have four seasons, each with its own rigid and immutable style, but rather a completely different look for each separate variation in climate or mood. Each style will be stylistically precise and complete, and since nature does not always in fact perform as per the precisions of date time and seasonal anticipations, one will be left with a choice of fashion to suit the mood both of nature and of oneself. Thus instead of four we shall have perhaps ten or even twelve styles to choose from and according to our own free will. The current fashion anarchy is merely a halfway stage towards this future evolution. As a realisation this could really put the *haute couture* business back into fashion with a big bang. Perhaps with the 'Now Look'. Mini skirts and maxi skirts were both derived from this trend, and unless *haute couture* is willing to make peace with it them the business will continue to hang on to the coat-tails of the younger generation for its ideas. Yves St. Laurent for example is at present giving the lead in this regard. He now goes to the Kings Road, Chelsea, for his ideas.

One cannot successfully fight against a natural social trend. Far better to extract the best from the often rather obscure idea underlying it, and come out one step ahead. Christian Dior did exactly this with his 'New Look' in 1947. At the end of the war years of clothes rationing and general austerity, he caught the public mood and cashed in on a winner. People were tired of privation and wanted to show their reaction against it. After having to scrimp and save coupons to buy a bare minimum of material to cover their necessity, they were suddenly presented with an abundance to choose from – and skirts went down, quite naturally. In most things there is cause and reaction, even in *haute couture*. It is this fine, clairvoyant, mixing of artistic effect with current trends in thought that keeps the genius of *haute couture* alive.

As I waited in the studio, I could see into the inner sanctum where Balmain was draping some gorgeous peacock-blue silk on Naomi, a fantastic creature from South Africa. The line that season appeared to be, from the side view, a kind of S-shape. From the shoulders, a dress was curved inwards in a sweep, coming forward around the hip bones, with a slight fullness over the tummy. *Je veux que ca creuse*, Balmain would say rolling his R's and waving his arms in an intensely graceful sweep. Naomi had the perfect shape for this line. She had suffered terribly from various chest ailments as a child, and, poor darling, was rather frail. But she had the most elegant round shoulders, no bosom at all, a long swan-like neck that came forward from her shoulders at an angle of forty-five degrees, hip bones like razor blades which joined on to long slim sparrow-like legs, and she was pale and out of this world. As she floated down the runway, you might think she would fall over one of her long elegant feet, as she peered unsmilingly through her droopy downward-pointing eye lashes. Balmain adored her and was very much inspired by her aura. Everyone adored her in fact, for underneath this bizarre and rather legendary exterior there was a woman with a fantastic sense of humour, just dying to get out.

I took careful note of Naomi's antics in the studio, and when my turn came to be fitted I stood in front of the mirrors sucking in my cheeks, pushing out my pelvis, and trailing my left leg languidly, while Raymond supported bales of cloth behind me and Eric and Balmain draped the unrolled ends of the bale over me, pinning sometimes into the cloth and sometimes into me. But I didn't mind suffering the pin pricks too much for this, my very first Balmain creation. It was an evening dress in rich wine-coloured velvet, draped over one shoulder, the other shoulder bare, with a straight wrap-over skirt; supremely elegant. They stood back to see the effect, talking together all the time, building each other up into a crescendo of creativity, whereupon Balmain leaped over the desk and quickly made a rough sketch. Then one of the fitters was called in, and *voila*, a dress was born.

Sometimes Balmain invents a dress directly on to paper, often talking and describing things meanwhile to Eric as he is busily working away with his pencil, and then again he very often works directly with the material on the mannequin to see what it suggests to him.

This is the time when the artistry of the mannequin comes into its own. An intense creative relationship is established at this point between the designer and the model girl. An intelligent girl knows just how to droop elegantly with her left hip forward or direct her elbow backwards, one wrist placed just so on her waist, where she happens to be holding up the skirt with one hand; and how to turn her body to an angle so that the designer cannot see the way the other hand is holding together the piece of cloth which is swathed round her head, an excess that may or may not end up as a turban. This is where she may subtly have her own influence on future designs and hem lengths. She may, for example, surreptitiously raise or lower the hemline at this rudimentary stage, or even play around with a fold of material by trying it this way or that, until something catches the eye of the designer and he will then capture the idea and establish it on paper. The bone structure, the colouring and the general air of a mannequin can indeed instigate a whole new fashion. Indirectly and most discreetly of course! It's the eternal sequence of woman expressing herself through her man; being a source of inspiration is, to my mind, the finest way for a woman to express and assert her sex.

Mannequins must be many things, but above all strange and interesting and never merely pretty. It is perhaps difficult to pay sufficient attention to the contours of the landscape if the sun is too distracting. She must express things with her body. Her face should be simply a facet of this total interest.

When the sketch has been handed over to the fitters it becomes their turn to show their ingenuity. Although extremely clever, it is comparatively rare for a fitter ever to graduate to becoming a designer herself. Most of them have been with the House of Balmain for years and know the work of the master very well. Consequently they are able to complete an outfit from a very simply sketched impression. There are about twelve fitters, each one in charge of an *atelier* or workroom consisting of forty girls. Certain fitters are best at coats and tailoring and others excel at evening and afternoon dresses, working in fine wools, silks and exquisite embroidery.

High on a shelf surrounding the central workroom stands an illustrious company of noble ladies, peering out over the concentrated activity. Their busts do anyway. These are the tailor's dummies of such eminent regular customers as Madame Suzy Volterra, The Duchess of Bedford, Baroness Rothschild, Marlene Dietrich etc. There they stand like rather unflattering effigies, with wads of extra padding here and there and pins and needles stuck into them. A superstitious African witch-doctor would be appalled.

The length of time it takes to make a dress depends I suppose upon Parkinson's law. A dress designed at the beginning of the *pose* is occasionally still being worked upon on the eve of press day. Having started off as a backless, frontless, sleeveless full length black chiffon, and then having been ripped apart about seventeen times, it has finally ended up as an entirely covered up, long-sleeved midi. One occasionally arrives at an interesting creation in this manner, though not often. The best things are those which are the result of creative lightning. In this way a suit will be conceived at 4 p.m. on Thursday and is ready to be shown to the press the following day, complete with buttons and button-holes plus the chic allure that makes a reputation. During the *pose* the lights of Balmain burn late and brightly and very often far into the night. Such a fever of excitement can only be compared to the theatre world, perhaps the opening of a new play when people feel themselves part of a conspiracy. Each one has his role to play and despite fierce, electric storms of temperament, everyone is very dedicated to the task ahead.

Dresses are carried from *atelier* to studio over the arms of little seamstresses, the precious creations being carefully concealed under covers. Only a select few may see the dress before Press Day. There is a big market for 'poached' designs, and a very heavy penalty for anyone caught stealing designs. From time to time it has been known that a photographer looking like an innocuous tourist has lurked outside 44 rue Francois I in the hopes of catching a glimpse of an original model as it flutters past the window. Quick as a flash he takes a picture, and subsequently sells it to a newspaper or a wholesale firm of model-copyists for a large sum. Once, a buyer hired a photographer who took up vigil in a room in the Bellman Hotel directly opposite, with his zoom lens poised at the ready. Fortunately he was seen before very long and the police were sent for. The Paris police have an entire department devoted to rag-trade robberies. Wherever there is big business there is always a little monkey business, and even I have been approached and offered an enormous sum of money to pass on a few useful titbits about line, length, and cut. Sheer uninspired audacity. Needless to say I would not dream of encouraging them in such a lack of imagination. Once the collection has been shown of course there is nothing to be done about poachers. They sit in the salon, often quite blatantly sketching certain models and memorising and copying details here and there. In order to prevent the complete disintegration of the business, an entrance fee is charged to all firms visiting the collection. This fee can be anything from £200 to £1,000 depending on the firm, and entitles them to the pattern or *toile* of one or two models. Private clients are, of course, allowed in free. Occasionally there are firms who pose as private clients so as to avoid paying the fee. But Madame Spanier, the dynamic *Directrice* of the salon, with her eagle eye, claims to be able to spot them immediately by their jewellery. Only rag-trade people flash around the latest 'rocks' on undistinguished hands, according to her. Private customers are generally wearing the family jewels in old-fashioned settings.

When Balmain had finished his first fitting on me I put on my white overall again and returned to the *cabine*. Some of the other mannequins had arrived and the old guard was busily eyeing the new guard with curiosity, and vice versa. Mannequins, I now know, are always absolutely fascinated by other mannequins.

There was Lina, the last of the really 'elegant lady' mannequins. She is Italian, but has been so long in France that she has adopted the same sort of chic that French women have. Balmain always says that she is his Michele Morgan, for she resembles the French film star closely. She loves to talk all the time as Italians are prone to do, and when there is no one around to understand her she talks to herself, giving a running commentary upon her every action. 'Now I shall brush my hair', 'I will powder my nose', 'I shall put on my earrings *et voila!*' Incessantly . . . in long sunny streams of verbal spaghetti. A charming completely innocent and elegant person.

Lina began as a mannequin with Piquet, and has become a kind of legend *chez Balmain*. No one knows her exact age, but Lina is timeless. She has her own particular style of showing, very slow, elegant and relaxed. Sometimes the younger mannequins get impatient with her for taking too long on the podium, and not flashing up and down like a bat out of hell as the rest of us do, in keeping with the modern trend. But Lina will just smile sweetly at her customers and then rake in her commission at the end of the month. For she has always sold more dresses than any of us. She knows most of the customers personally and they all know her by name. Lina will welcome them like a hostess to her garden party, smiling with her eyes.

There was also Rosemary, a German girl married to a

Frenchman. All the mannequins envied Rosemary because she had such tiny hips and slim thighs, and an enormous and perfectly shaped bosom. But alas the mannequins were alone in their appreciation, for Balmain hates bosoms! All the designers do, as a matter of fact. They spoil the line of the clothes, ruin the cut, and bulge in all the places where you should cave in, according to them. Thus women with shapely bosoms are seldom considered chic, and Rosemary had a not very aesthetic flattening-out bust-bodice constructed for her, which was specifically designed to smooth away any telltale signs of ultra-femininity. (A girdle worn around the chest does just as well if you feel the urge for that kind of chic.)

There were eight mannequins altogether, Petra (dark haired and rather intense), also hailed from Germany; Danielle, the only French girl, was very slim, tiny and elegant. For some reason French girls, though chic, seldom seem to make it in the *haute couture.* On the other hand you don't have to be French to be a Parisienne. Paris is made up of all nationalities. The *haute couture* turns you into a Parisienne, and strangely enough those Parisiennes who are successful seem to be of Polish, Hungarian or yet some other extraction. Swedes and Russians also seem to make very good 'Parisiennes'.

Balmain likes to employ foreign girls, particularly English or American. American girls have a chic all of their own. They are so professional in their work, and they always have such beautiful slim legs and elegant feet.

But the mannequin that impressed me the most, on that first morning at Balmain, was a model I will call Victoria. She arrived like a whole crowd, having come straight to work from a night-long round of Paris night spots and champagne orgies, finishing up with pickled herrings and two pints of larger to insulate her hangover. Victoria's jet-black hair had been cut off to a one-inch length all over, and she wore it brushed straight back like a man's. Her nose was large, and she had a large bright-scarlet mouth, and a laugh that sounded like a depraved hyena. In fact the most striking thing about her was that she was always twice as much of everything. Everything about her was carried to sublime excess; her strong sense of drama appealed to them at Balmain, and apart from finding her an endless source of amusement, they liked to dress her in the most positive colours. A black velvet trouser-suit, a full-length white ermine evening dress, or crimson silk crêpe. Stunningly dramatic.

Despite the crazy life that Victoria led, and the incredible incidents, dramas and crises that overtook her every now and then (her love life was an open book), she was an extremely consciencious worker, and never once did she arrive late for work or drooping from lack of sleep. If ever we had an early morning rendezvous at the airport for 5 o'clock, when taking off *en masse* on one of our frequent lightning trips, Victoria was always the first to arrive, all ready and made up, just in case there was a photographic send-off. The rest of us would arrive white and shaking, wearing the inevitable pair of dark glasses in order to cover the match-sticks propping open our minds.

Victoria hailed from a very poor and notoriously rough neighbourhood of Paris, and though she no longer lived there herself she paid frequent visits to see her *petite mere*, whom she adored. Sometimes she would bring this little old lady along to watch the collection being shown, reserving for her the place of honour in the salon. Victoria was a hell raiser. She had streams of lovers and ex-lovers whom she treated atrociously. There were always bouquets of flowers and presents arriving for her and once a young man came bearing an anguished expression and a knife! Fortunately for her there was a way out of the back door.

It was Victoria who had the hair that Balmain wished upon all of us for that season. A few days later the hairdressers arrived for a conference about styles. Alexandre is the biggest hairdresser in Paris; his list of clients includes half the nobility of Europe (including Elizabeth Taylor who is after all practically royalty herself these days). Alexandre is short, dark, loud and vociferous and has an entourage of equally short, dark, loud followers who stand around snipping and spraying and baring their teeth. Balmain becomes very switched-on when they are around, and they all go off into a huddle to the inner-most-inner sanctum and one by one the mannequins are called in and are given the chop as it is called, or occasionally in rare cases a reprieve – when, for example, a girl has fainted with horror at the thought of cutting off all the long hair that she has been proudly growing since the age of five. But more often than not they are utterly ruthless.

The following day I found myself ensconced in one of Alexandre's plush seats surrounded by potted ferns and Cocteau originals and phonies, whilst several beautiful young men handed me on from one to another. (One super-exquisite creature even sported a most becoming set of false eyelashes.) Six hours later, I emerged from this garden of delights minus my patience and nearly all my hair. What little remained was lacquered severely back behind my ears à la Victoria, and coloured a deep ranch-mink colour.

'I suppose I'll get used to it', I thought to myself as I dodged and parried a few last minute snips from Alexandre, 'but I shall have to change my personality to match it!' M. Balmain thought it was *ravissante*. Monsieur Eric too, and everyone echoed these sentiments ardently. Meanwhile I comforted myself with the thought that at least my head had not been shaved, as had that of one of the mannequins at Yves St. Laurent. Designers usually dislike hair. It detracts from the line, and therefore they like hair to be as simple and clear-cut as possible. This creates a great conflict between the designers and the hairdressers, as of course hairdressers prefer something elaborate in order to show off their skill.

Balmain is rather more on the side of the hat manufacturers. He has a wonderful old lady called Madame le Gros who is covered in jewels and who is in charge of the hat department. She makes delicious hats with anything and everything. But in actual fact I notice that few women in Europe wear hats any more, especially since the hairdressing boom. French women, especially, hardly ever wear hats. In England, women over a certain age wear them, and German women wear them in the afternoons whilst eating cream cakes. The real mad-hatter's haven of the western world is America.

But personally, I am on the side of the hairdressers, since I think that hats are very ageing, and I also think that the most important part of dressing is one's hair; the cut, colour, and quality. Hair should be very well cut, if it is short, and simply arranged, and not tinted – unless there are grey hairs, and then a tint lifts the years off. I prefer hair long, being a romantic, or else very, very short. But then one needs very large eyes, a wide mouth, and tiny bones to look really appealingly feminine à la Hepburn (Audrey) and the Mia Farrow style.

Balmain's ideal of womanhood was the late Kay Kendal. He often cited her as a perfect example of true elegance. He designed the wardrobe for many of her films. One season we all had our hair cut like hers, brushed back behind the ears and up at the back with curls on top, which necessitated a permanent wave for most of us. But in fact though this may have looked very sophisticated, for some reason curls appear to me to be very ageing on the younger woman. Perhaps they should be accompanied by the dignity of age. Curls seem to be to peg every woman's age at fifty. I think smooth sleek hair looks much more distinguished on the younger girl-about-town.

During that first week at Balmain, I began to feel cosseted and important and star-like. My image was changing and I learnt how to get 'hung-up' on that image in the mirror; I used to spend hours preening and perfecting it.

One day Monsieur Nicolet from Revlon arrived, and designed a new face for us all. Each of us was given a complete range of beauty products including the very latest innovations. Eyes were to be large, haunting and Garboesque – that is, drooping downwards at the corners, with silver-white on the lids and dark-brown shading under the eye-bone and halfway down the inside of the nose bone. A whole gamut of eye shadows was used in this prototype face, from pink, for underneath the eyebrows, to yellow ochre, on the outer corners of the lids. (I always thought 'pink eye' was a disease that belonged to rabbits!) Then we had our eyebrows plucked to two thin lines and brushed upwards, and the hairs stuck in position with soap, as apparently Sophia Loren does with hers. Our lips were outlined in a dark red pencil and filled in with the colour that they were pushing that season. Finally came the cheek-bones. A liberal supply of rouge was applied as shading under the bone, which was highlighted with a streak of silver white on top. When Monsieur Nicolet had finished his demonstration we were asked to copy the original under his supervision. The effects that we achieved when let loose on our own faces were quite remarkable, if nothing else. In fact the person who finally gazed back at me from my mirror was completely alien to me. 'I expect I shall get used to her too', I told myself as I smoothed back my hair. But then I turned to look at Christine, a myopic brunette from Poland. She generally wore a pair of large tinted spectacles except when she was showing the collection, when she just had to rely on her sixth sense to tell her where the end of the runway was, or maybe her eyelashes acted as antennae of a kind. But in order to make up her eyes she had first to remove her glasses, then she would carefully draw some lines, then replace her spectacles so as to see where she had put the lines. But by this time she couldn't see them anyway since they were covered by the glasses. The final

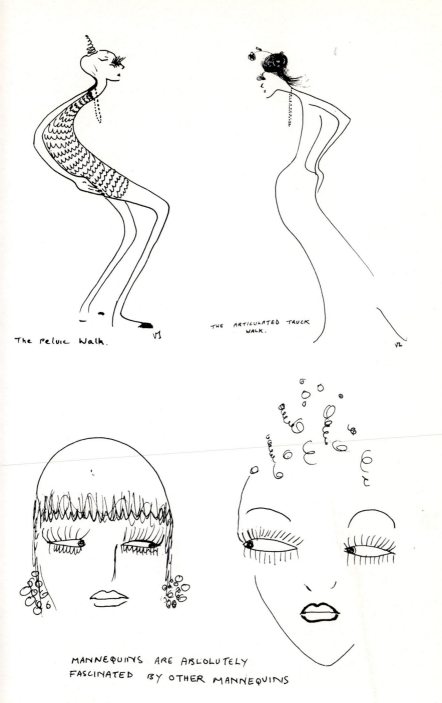

The Pelvic Walk.

THE ARTICULATED TRUCK WALK.

MANNEQUINS ARE ABSOLUTELY
FASCINATED BY OTHER MANNEQUINS

Some of my impressions of the way mannequins walk and look

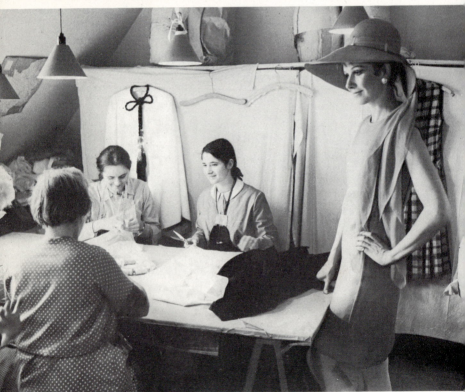

Above. Putting on my hat in front of the composite mirror in the *cabine*
Below. With the girls in the workroom

effect looked rather like Mickey Mouse with a hangover. Poor Christine! She did a lot to keep the *cabine* happy.

The strange thing is that women are all convinced that they look much better with make-up on, but I have yet to meet the man who likes make-up on women. The men I know won't even tolerate mascara, and as for lipstick, that is complete anathema to them. Most of them are only concerned with how you look underneath the camouflage. This doesn't seem to stop women being fascinated by make-up though and make-up firms being fascinated by women. And I must say it is amazing what changes can be made in a face when make-up is cleverly applied. It is fun to change ones look; and of course it is certainly nothing new for women to paint themselves – I'll bet Cleopatra would have adored the Jean Harlow look. It takes some mannequins about two hours to apply their make-up perfectly, and I have been known to take that long too, although being an inveterate last minute arriver I have now mastered the art of doing it in four minutes flat, and am able to transform those two beady black-currants into large limpid pools full of expression (to coin a cliché) in record time.

Every season we get new eyes. Sometimes they are round, and sometimes they are long, and sometimes triangular, and once we even had to wear eyelashes on the lower lids as well as the top, applied individually. If you laughed too hard you could find a clump of lashes clinging to your cheek like a rather embarrassing hairy wart. But then mannequins are not supposed to laugh! At least not whilst they are showing. Too much animation tends to make people look at your face instead of at the clothes, therefore a vacant stare tinged with disdain is commonly adopted on the podium. But you really should get a glimpse behind the scenes sometimes. Nervous tension is responsible for a lot of it. Of course we have to be awfully careful not to let the customers hear any hysterical hilarity; and Maggie makes more noise than all of us put together telling us to be quiet. So we try silent laughing. The best silent laugher I have ever known was Marina. With her high forehead, straight black hair scraped severely back, and perfectly classical features, Marina was the epitome of sophisticated aloofness. But I have seen her stand rooted to the spot with her mouth wide open for a full four minutes, unable to move and not making a sound, just quaking with laughter.

It is not always the sound of laughter, however, that has to be kept from the customers. Sometimes a bloodcurdling row will break out between two mannequins, over a hat or a pair of shoes or something equally trivial. 'You are wearing my hat, and your head is bigger than mine, and you will stretch it. Take it off!' 'Your head is so small because all you have in there is a pea!' 'And yours is full of potatoes, melons.' Screech. And other such frank and scintillating observations.

One of my first fittings was for an evening dress. I saw the sketch of it, and it was white Ziberline with the bodice and the hem encrusted with the most fabulously intricate jewels, blue and silver in the shape of flowers with droplet pearls hand sewn all over. The cut was simple, but the materials were ravishing; I felt like a queen when I wore it at the rehearsal on Friday. The dress was called *Tour d'Argent*.

Rehearsals begin about 6 o'clock in the evening and invariably drag on for hours and hours, sometimes until midnight, during which time the mannequins are kept alive on an unstinted supply of the finest champagne, high octane fuel for high-powered race horses. We stand there, pose, walk around, pose and just stand, for hours, while Balmain, Eric, and Raymond scrutinise every detail under the harsh glare of the salon lighting. Sometimes they hurl insults and sometimes verbal bouquets. Sometimes, a dress that has started off upon one mannequin will be switched to another. Perhaps it looks completely different on the new mannequin; she may radiate that indefinable something that was previously lacking. Then of course – and almost invariably – the previous mannequin feels thoroughly dejected, will not speak to the one who now has 'her' dress, and may well end up in tears. It is always a tricky situation. Mannequins are super-sensitive egoistic creatures and nearly always take it as a personal affront.

Once I was given a dress that had originally been created for Tania. It was a long white crêpe, exquisitely simple, with a floating panel from shoulder to hem. Tania told me sweetly how happy she was for me, that it looked much better on me and that it had practically been her idea to change mannequins. As I stepped onto the podium to show it, however, I heard a horrible tearing sound and was stuck rooted to the spot feeling an idiot. Someone had 'accidentally' caught the floating panel in the door!

Last seasons favourite mannequin may be this seasons also-ran, and the new beauties get all the fuss and attention. It gave me the necessary ego-fodder I needed to start with. I was a new girl. My photo, which had been taken countless times already, was taken some more. I had been interviewed by most of the *British* press and was already booked to appear on the B.B.C., I.T.V., C.B.S., N.B.C., and goodness knows what else. There seemed to be no limits anymore, and absolutely anything could happen, it seemed. This was a magic land.

Returning home at night, Hen, Fifi and I used to collapse, taking it in turns to soak our aching feet in the bidet, too exhausted even to eat. Hen and Fifi were going through similar scenes *chez Lanvin*. We had lots of notes to compare, and it was such fun recounting the day's events to each other, usually over a plate of courgettes or a raw carrot and a hard-boiled egg, (my staple diet when I'm not dining out on oysters and champagne). It seemed as though the whole of Paris was bursting with a golden secret, a secret to which we were privileged to hold the key.

As the time for Press Day draws near, the pace hots up and

passions mount in intensity. The working day lasts longer and tempers grow shorter. Press Day is always held on the last Tuesday in July or January. On every Friday rehearsal, more and more dresses have been added. I had about eighteen outfits to present. My favourite turned out to be the most expensive item in the whole collection. It was a coat of that most luxurious, exotic, and feminine of furs – Chinchilla.

When the coat first materialised there was some doubt and consternation about it. Often Balmain likes to have a customer in mind when he designs something, particularly when the item happens to be priced at £15,000. Carol Baker, he decided was a natural for the chinchilla. She quite often shopped at Balmain. But there was something not quite right about it as he, and then Eric and Raymond, surveyed it super-critically in the studio. We were all standing there enviously watching as Rosemarie paraded around presenting the chinchilla. 'Victoria!' shouted Balmain suddenly. 'This coat needs Victoria!' Her face lit up, and in a flash and a flurry she had the coat on and was caressing it sensuously. Eric's nostrils however were twitching haughtily. 'It looks vulgar' he hissed, turning away. (The crime of crimes in the *haute couture*). 'Then Naomi must wear it', said Balmain, as Victoria's smile turned to ice. Naomi drooped up and down the studio clutching feebly at the coat. But she looked as though she were drowning in it. So they passed it on to Tania, Danielle then Marina, and to each mannequin in turn, until finally Balmain said 'What about Lady Bread and Butter?' 'What indeed,' echoed Eric dispiritedly. Raymond helped me into the beautiful fur. Balmain perused it for a while and then said, 'Let's see how it looks in the salon'. And amid 'Alarums and escurscions' a solemn procession, headed by Balmain followed by Eric, with me and 'the coat' in the middle, and Raymond beating a metaphorical tattoo with a pair of chop sticks bringing up the rear, wended its way down to the salon. The lights went up and I went into my number.

On my second 'slink' up the catwalk, I allowed the coat to fall open and gradually off one shoulder. On the *fromage* (the round part where we do our turns) I let it drop onto the floor – then catching it by the scruff of the neck, I walked off, dragging it along the carpet behind me, with the very blankest expression that I could indolently muster. 'Oh; she dragged it', exclaimed Eric. 'She dragged it' echoed Raymond. 'But of course' said Balmain excitedly. 'It takes an Englishwoman to wear furs with such casual elegance!'

So the coat became mine, and I wore it with a long black velvet sheath with no back. 'Rich Beat-Nick', purred Balmain contentedly.

Later on, during a trip to Stockholm to present the collection before the King and Queen, a photo of me appeared in a Swedish newspaper with a caption which read (a free translation from the Swedish), 'The richest bitch in the world! Could you afford her?' Apart from the top-to-toe Balmain clothes, including the famous chinchilla, I was also wearing a fabulous diamond watch plus a pair of exquisite little earpieces which alone were worth around £25,000; and decked with this treature, there I was leaning on a gold-plated custom-built Rolls-Bentley which had silk seats and genuine Persian rugs on the floor, and which had cost around £30,000. The whole ensemble, car included, must have come to a cool mmmmmmmmmmmmmmmmmmmm, which roughly translated means in excess of £125,000.

The car, incidentally, belonged to a half-Viennese, half-Chinese Prince whom I met at a reception in the Royal Palace and who later pursued me to Paris. But that's another story.

The Chinchilla turned out to be more of a white elephant and was still around at the end of the season. Carol Baker had preferred the good old blonde-mink sex-symbol, and there remained the problem of what to do with it. 'I think we'll have to turn it into a block of flats!' said Eric absurdly; and in fact it did turn up next season as a jacket, the following season as a stole, and finally finished up as collars and cuffs.

The last Friday rehearsal is reserved for the expert, critical, observations of the well-known T.V. personality who is also the Sales Directrice of the House of Balmain, Madame Ginette Spanier. Madame Spanier is one of those positive thinkers. She is also a professional appreciator, and adored by creative people. Her tremendous and genuine enthusiasm is indeed invaluable and essential to them, in order to extract the best from their talent. She sits in the salon at Balmain's right hand looking expensive, chic, and elegant, exuding perfume and magic, and lacing her opinions with a completely unabashed use of superlatives. If she doesn't like an outfit, she says nothing. If she likes it she exclaims, 'How divine!' and if she sees something that she knows is going to sell over and over again she positively shrieks, 'Bread and butter! Bread and butter with jam on it!'

Balmain and she sometimes disagree about certain things, but more often than not he listens to her practical comments with regard to saleability. For example, sometimes there are not enough evening dresses in the collection with simple necklines that will show off the family jewels. Obviously dresses which are already heavily encrusted are unsuitable for this purpose. Or then again, there may be too few afternoon dresses with elaborate necklines. For this type of dress sells well to wealthy ladies who spend the greater part of their lives semi-hidden behind a bridge table.

After the rehearsal, it has become a tradition that Madame Spanier, Balmain, Eric, and Raymond dine together at a chic restaurant down in *Les Halles*, where they discuss the collection and make last-minute changes and improvements, Balmain sketching designs and noting ideas on the tablecloth. Then the entire weekend is passed at fever-pitch, with more fittings on Saturday. On Sunday morning the show that Balmain likes least takes place: the special preview for the *vendeuses*. They frequently make a dour and difficult audience. Terrified of new trends or revolutionary hem-lengths, however beautiful they may be, their main and over-riding concern is, 'Can I sell it?' Perhaps commission-based salaries are responsible for their conservative attitude. Whatever the reason, they fill the salon with an anxious silence and cause Balmain to become nervous and intro-spective. Their eyes flicker like cash registers. They applaud faintly at the end, and mutter ominously amongst them-selves. They are so devastatingly critical of the clothes, the hats, the hairstyles, the shoes and of course the mannequins – but, oh so lacking in fantasy! However, their part in the financial success of the Balmain outfit is indispensable, and much of their sales-technique is based upon a genuine desire to see their customers looking chic and elegant and feeling happy with their purchases. In fact, when they are not with a client most of them are warm, charming people who happen to be doing a rather exacting job.

On Monday there are more fittings, and last-minute changes, and switches around, and bouts of hysteria and tears and frayed nerves. There is one more sneak preview before zero hour, this time to a V.I.P. audience of ambassadors and their wives and various nobs and snobs (short for *nobilité* and *sine nobilité*[1]). The guest-list on such occasions is sprinkled with names such as Rothchild, Duff-Cooper, Soames, and Salinger, there is the Comptesse de Vigny and Baron le Batard the Earl of Litchfield (and even Lord Abraham Salt Beef himself, canned as usual). A graciously elite and appreciative audience, compared to the *vendeuses*. But then they can afford to be. The street outside is littered with Rolls-Royces and Cadillacs, and liveried chauffeurs, helping ancient peers and peeresses from the comfortable cushiony depths of their limousines.

After the champagne-and-caviar reception, an intelligent mannequin goes home to grab some beauty sleep for tomorrow's big day when she will become practically a

[1] *Sine* is Latin for 'without'.

commodity along with the clothes that she is showing. (At least I am sure that's the way we appear to the press). But somehow or other I became accustomed to getting very little sleep, Paris night-life and invitations being so tempting, and in fact I ended the day of my first 'in show' to the Monday elite by making a hectic night-club circuit with one of my interviewers who was doing a T.V. programme about fashion. Thus the historic moment arrived, and Press Day dawned with a horrible thud. I was hung-over. When the clock in the *cabine* stayed still long enough for me to orientate, it said 8.15, and I fought my way to my place through a throng of people who all had perfectly legitimate reasons for being there. There seemed to be at least 2,000 people all in the *cabine* at once. In fact there must have been about sixty. It reminded me a little of the American college game of trying to see how many people you can cram into a telephone-box. First there were we mannequins and our dressers, then there were all twelve fitters and their seconds, on guard in case of still further last-minute adjustments to their creations. There were the hairdressers brandishing curling-tongs and lacquer sprays, by far the most dangerous people there. There were the make-up experts wielding paint-brushes dripping with great gobs of yellow-brown eye shadow. There were the hat ladies, the shoe gentlemen, and Raymond, Eric and Monsieur Balmain. Not to mention a team of T.V. cameramen with their cameras, cables and paraphernalia to fall over and into, plus a couple of legitimate press photographers trying to get candid shots of us with or without our bras.

Balmain was quiet and somewhat nervous but not without his sense of humour. One mannequin was not feeling well and sat with her head cradled in her hands, sobbing quietly 'What's the matter darling', he asked. 'I feel horrible', she sobbed. 'Oh is that all' he laughed, and added 'You should have been a boy, like me!' This last remark must have triggered off something, for the mannequin recovered herself sufficiently to totter to her feet and reply with a twinge of exasperation, 'Monsieur Balmain, I will change my hair for you, I will change my face for you and I will even change my name for you, but never will I change my sex!' And with that, she stalked out of the cabine and was never seen nor heard of again. Silly girl. No humour.

Zero hour is at ten and the count-down starts around nine o'clock. Just then the make-up man sees me trapped and unable to move, held in the iron grip of a pair of curling-tongs which are dangerously close to my right ear; he dives at me with his yellow paint-brush and I have no alternative but to let him have his head, especially as the 'madame hats' is busily trying to cram a kind of 'Borscht Circuit' special onto mine. Maggey the *chef* stands in the middle of it all, shouting and directing the traffic around her — like a Parisian *flic* — with a mad look in her eye.

The dresses hang silently on their rails above our heads out of harm's way. The only time the crowd will part is when one of the dressers gallops through the creative throng wielding a dangerous looking *yoyo* (a long pole with a hook on the end of it), in order to spear down a dress, with a wild cry of *attention les plumes!*

There is the faint lingering perfume of garlic in the air as I gaze at this strange being in the mirror who once was me and is now beginning to take on a legendary air. Naomi is having a swig of cognac from her secret cache under one of the hats. She passes me the bottle. Not too much, or the press will be writing about the original new-style walk that the Paris mannequins have this season. Nine-fifteen and someone is tugging at my elbow. I turn and see a mouth saying something. It's one of the fitters and she wants me to try on one of her suits as she thought she saw a lurk in the sleeve yesterday. '*Non, non, non,*' I cry, becoming suddenly more French than the French. I think I am going out of my mind. The heat is incredible and my make-up feels as though it's running into my eyes. Nine-twenty-five, and oh my God! I have forgotten to scratch the soles of my new shoes and I can hardly stand up in them they are so slippery. A hasty operation with the points of a pair of scissors makes them safer for cornering. Nine-thirty and I manage to get my eyebrows stuck down and fix on two pairs of false lashes. My face is rather round, so I use a lot of shading about the cheekbones. One side of my hair is done, and I hope he will leave it at that as I have hats with my first few outfits in any case, so no hair will be showing. Nine-thirty-five and I put my hat on first and stand up, providing a magnificent target for those wretched photographers. So I throw a temperament and they are put out, which makes two less bodies using up the precious air in the *cabine*.

My dresser holds out my first outfit, a wintery brown and black tweed suit. But first I climb into three pairs of tights and a pair of black shiny boots. Wearing all my tights at once saves time changing. Then, feeling a trifle stiff-legged, I step into the tweed suit. It has a high collar and blouse underneath, not to mention the matching top coat which has a solid mink lining. (That means three turns up and down the runway.) Nine thirty-five and I am all zipped and buttoned and a hairdresser is preening my fringe whilst I edge towards the exit onto the podium where *le patron* is standing waiting to give that final adjustment. This generally means that he rams the hat down further over your eyes, removes the earrings that you have chosen and replaces them with another identical pair, makes you put your gloves on instead of carrying them, and tells you that you look like last years winner of the Tour de France. Then I see Madame Spanier's special announcing shoes placed next to the microphone, and I know that we are nearly there. It is the tradition that Madame Spanier always announces for the press show in French and English every season. And for good luck she always wears a pair of little jewelled slippers that were given to her by Claudette Colbert. Mannequins are lining up ready for blast-off now, and inspecting their stockings in the long mirror. Some are introspective and quiet, and others are having last-minute scraps about something. But one sure thing is that we step through that curtain we are all going to look cool, exotic, and untouchable.

And then Balmain is hissing 'Lady Bread and Butter' at me and prodding me in the back saying *'Merde! Merde!'* (I later discovered this to be a good-luck saying in French *bouture* and show biz circles). And suddenly there I am through to the other side of the curtain. I pause for an instant and take in the sea of faces. The salon is literally all a flutter with jangly fashion editoresses squeezing in between their dead-lines. They are all fanning themselves with the programme in an effort to combat the almost intolerable heat, and some people even carry portable electric fans.

Not only is the salon so bursting with people that they seem to be hanging from the ceiling, but the passage is lined on either side with them, and all the fitting rooms are taken over, and even the staircase is crammed with faces and photographers.

Fashion editoresses are a rare and exotic species somewhat astringent in their outlook on life. They represent a formid-able battery of critics and frequently appear to be rather eccentric. The sea of faces that greets my debut has a character all its own!

I step out boldly, me and all my mink, make it to the *fromage*, turn, and present myself to the sea of glittering eyes. Then back I walk hoping that I'll get all my buttons undone in time. I just make the last button before I spin round with a flourish and whip open the coat, revealing the mink lining. A gasp of surprise from the audience, for what looked like a rather sensible winter coat now has another side to its nature. Down the runway once more, slowly removing the coat and showing the matching suit beneath. I try to slip the jacket off gracefully on my next run, but it gets stuck on my gloves so I have to pretend that I meant it to. The main thing is not to lose your cool when you can't get a button undone, or you nearly lose a shoe on the runway, or when perhaps you spin around too fast and all but fall flat on your face. Sometimes by extending the accident until it appears to be done on purpose, one achieves that stroke of originality bordering on genius.

Now I have to go through the same routine in the passage-way, and all the other spaces where people are squeezed in, picking my way between the legs and dodging the hands that try to get a feel of the cloth as I pass. It's difficult to spin round, especially when the dress has large floating sleeves for example, without sweeping off with the hairpiece, spectacles, and all the notes of one of the clients.

Then at last I return to the *cabine*, where everything is ripped off me in two seconds flat, and the hairdressers launch a new offensive whilst I button up a navy-blue and brown suit (Balmain's favourite colour combination) and feel around with my foot for a shoe, and the *patron* clips an earring on, and the mafia are going at my hair with the lacquer spray as once again I waft through the curtain, gliding along on a miasma of heat and a cocktail of different perfumes and hearing the low hum of humanity on the verge of hysteria.

After the suits, the afternoon dresses, the 'little black numbers', the furs, and then finally we arrive at the highlight of the collection – the evening dresses, where a designer can really indulge his fantasies. As each dress is shown a burst of applause celebrates its impact, and each dress seems to surpass the one before, culminating in heavily-jewelled, encrusted gowns such as one might see worn by the Queen at a Royal Command Performance.

I make a stately entrance in my very last dress. It is called 'Chopin'; a shocking-pink satin with pearls and crystals covering the bodice and round the hem. I feel exhilarated and

breathless and out of this world. . . . My hair, somehow or
other, is scraped back, and in no time an elaborate postiche
has been placed on top. The applause is exciting and
suddenly I feel so radiantly happy. 'This is your last dress', I
congratulate myself as I finally leave the podium, 'and you've
made it all through without tripping over your dress,
eye-lashes, or your new shoes, and no one even seemed to
notice your knees shaking or your eyelid twitching'. Now
there is only the famous Balmain wedding-dress to be shown.
It is worn by Danielle, looking fresh, demure, and innocent.
Who would ever guess that in real life she had three children
and was married to her second husband! Returning to the
cabine, Balmain too is elated, and everybody is hugging and
kissing everybody else, and Balmain says we are all *ravissante*
and *divine*, and hugs us each in turn; and a few mannequins
cry, and champagne explodes and froths all over the *cabine*,
and Balmain hugs us all again, and the cameras flash, and the
roof rises up, and I feel like singing, and as far as my mind
can see at that moment it seems like the whole world has
gone crazy. Outside in the passage there is an undignified
scramble as fashion correspondents rush off to phone their
write-ups to their editors. Some of them have artists in tow,
and frantically try to grab the dresses they want plus a
mannequin to pose whilst a lightning sketch is made.
Photographs are withheld from publication in the press until
one month has passed, to allow time for fashion firms to get
an exclusive view of the collection. Thus the fashion artists
come into their own, working with the press this time.
Sometimes they are so frantic to get a certain dress that
another fashion writer is also after that they almost come to
blows. They pay cash to the mannequin (30 or 50 francs) for
three or four minutes work.

By this time those mannequins who are not posing have
stripped off all but their bras and girdles and are collapsed
with their feet up on the dressing table. Their role is over for

the time being, so there they recline like fallen leaves or weary butterflies, their heads reeling with the echoes of applause, and perfectly satisfied with their brief moment of glory.

There are some things that one can get used to, however magical that might at first seem; but that initial first night first time magic of launching a 'collection' is new every time.

6

AFTER HOURS

After the Press Show and all the fittings are over, Pierre Balmain seeks refuge at his beautiful villa on the island of Elba. He suffers, like most creative artists, from finding only very rarely that longed-for response to his dream children, and he finds the first few days after the launching much too agonizing. Meanwhile the mannequins have to cope with a further two weeks of ruthless prodding and poking by buyers from dress manufacturers who, as I have already mentioned, have paid a lot of money for the privilege of copying one or two models and pinching a few ideas from the master mind. The buyers are, as they would be the first to tell you, very important people. They account for a large percentage of the revenue of an *haute couture* house. They usually want to examine the goods from close up before making their final purchase; and in consequence the mannequin has to be at work at nine in the morning for the first two weeks to cope with the rush, and to stand patiently in the salon whilst the thin, fat, short, lanky, well-dressed, overdressed, over-loud overlords scrutinize and dissect, the well-tuned beady business eye sharp as an eagle for the tastiest morsel, the latest fashion titbits, those little astute touches that can elevate a dress from the mundane and turn it into a *robe*. The salon begins to take on the ambiance of an Arab market place, with hoards of people muttering to each other in many different languages and tall mannequins standing inanely in the centre of a group amidst piles of gorgeous dresses, suits, and furs, scattered irreverently around the place. This, need I add, is the part that the mannequin enjoys least of all.

Sometimes buyers try to lure a mannequin away by offering her a large wad of money to come and work for them instead, usually in some such exotic place as Kansas City or a genuine Turkish bazaar. Some clients do become particularly tiresome, delighting in causing friction wherever they go. They love to bitch about the mannequins and about the clothes and the prices and the *vendeuses*, and I believe they really feel that they have scored when a fiery *vendeuse* finally blows her top, as the French are prone to do only too easily. Even so, mannequins have their own subtle ways of getting back at customers. A flap in the face from a heavy wide satin sleeve, or a pirouette just a little too close, blowing the contents of an ashtray into the eyes of the offensive one, or a stray hook at the end of a fur stole entangled in the chignon, the girl proceeding nonchalantly onward as though nothing had happened. Girls will be girls I suppose. Even mannequins.

On one particular occasion, though, the tables were really turned. I entered wearing a delicious, or so I thought, lime-green silk chiffon evening dress; a gorgeous creation. One particular customer, a large fat waist-coated man, seemed mesmerized. His eyes bulged — and then he threw up! I was devastated. So evidently was he. Probably a sleepless week of Paris night-clubbing hadn't much helped his artistic criticism. Paris night-clubs, if one has the stamina, can be rather alluring as I know.

If you've never been to Castels, you really have to go there just once in your life to believe it. At collection time it is the rendezvous of all the most beautiful and exotic-looking girls in the world. It's rather hard for outsiders to get in, I suppose; not that you have to be a member as such, but you are obliged to have that special something about you that says you are *dans le vent*, 'hip', 'yay yay', 'in' or whichever term you happen to like. If you conform to the required nonconformity, then you are permitted to insert yourself through the tiny doorway crammed with people, to pass through the upper bar, where you are not invited to linger unless you are 'super in' and Monsieur Castel himself suggests it, and thence down a cramped, narrow, hot, steamy, dark staircase into the small, low-ceilinged, low-lighted, low-down dive of heaving bodies, gyrating around to the sounds of the Stones, the Who, the What or Whichever, played at ultra-high decibel amplitude. It has a fabulous ambiance and I adore Castels. It was a kind of measure of a mannequin's popularity, how many times she was in Castels that week. I once managed twelve nights in a row. (That Olympic Marathon thing is strictly for sissies.) Most of the beautiful girls that one sees there are visiting Paris for a two-week photographic gig, being photographed by many of the top fashion photographers of the world, sporting the latest innovations for inclusion in the big glossies like Vogue, Harpers, Queens, and so on.

Much of this photographic work is carried on under cover of darkness; the clothes are not generally available for photographs until night falls, since during the day they are being shown to customers. Therefore the photographic model's day begins at around 6.30 p.m. and often continues until dawn. Those who finish work around one or two in the morning usually finish up at Castels to unwind a little, with photographer in tow. The first time I went there I met no end of photographers whom I knew from London, and we were all terribly impressed with each other. Looking around at the scene down there it seemed to me that the truly 'hip' model girl, with the most exquisite face and body, appeared to have chosen the ugliest creature she could find for a partner, often shorter than herself and dressed like an effeminate dog's bed. Certainly the opposite of the 'cover boy' she would probably have been photographed with that same day. It is true that most models are unanimous in their aversion to male models. They can't stand the competition, and rarely have anything to do with them outside working hours. One big ego is enough in a relationship. Or is it that some girls are so vain as to prefer a foil to their beauty, rather than a masculine complement? Perhaps it's a 'beauty and the beast' complex – or is it yet another part of a beautiful woman's most mysterious mystery? The 64,000 cent question.

One rather fantastic-looking 'girl' with long Nordic blonde hair and a pale delicate complexion, looking as fragile as a piece of Dresden china was rumoured to have been the homosexual drag queen of a famous West European city. But that's another sort of mystery which is beyond my comprehension. Some months later, after seeing this 'girl' at Castels, I was doing a special show of Balmain creations at a sumptuous restaurant in Paris when who should I find seated right next to me at the same dressing table but this very same person, so I was able to observe her discreetly close up. I concluded, after taking in all the pertinent details as it were, from navel to nostril, that the rumours just had to be false. You may imagine my surprise when a few moments later, as the pace hotted up, a voice something like a cross between Lee Marvin and a buzz saw hissed angrily in my ear, 'Darling, you have my shoes on'. I turned and saw the blonde beauty standing behind me, wearing a rather dangerous smile, whereupon I hastily kicked off the shoes and in my confusion went on barefoot. After all, he, she, or it, was bigger than both of us.

Hen, Fifi and I, meanwhile, were finding out all about Frenchmen. I accepted a blind date for the *quatorze juillet* with a Rothschild. (Well who wouldn't.) There were six of us in the party; three couples, that is. Myself and another model from Balmain, another girl, and three boys. They picked me up at our apartment in two cars, a sleek grey Citroen and a

Ferrari, and we all went off to La Coupole for dinner. Paris was in full swing when we left the restaurant, with people dancing in the streets, throwing streamers, and kissing each other. My Rothschild and I and the other couple were in the Citroen being driven by a tall Frenchman called Guy de something-or-other. (A 'de', by the way, is the French equivalent to the double-barrelled name of upper-class white Anglo-Saxons, and goes down very well with head waiters and the like.)

A race now began between Guy in the Citroen and the other couple in the Ferrari, and we literally burnt up the Boulevard Raspail. As we were side by side, held up at some traffic lights amid much laughing and shouting and swearing, the other driver wound down his window to shout some ribaldry at Guy, and quickly wound it up again. Just as well for him for Guy de . . ., spat and a great gob of spittle hit the window of the other car and ran slowly down. I was devastated and thought it absolutely revolting, and began to dislike the company intensely, but I decided to remain polite and see the thing through. That old British obstinate stoicism. My escort seemed to me, though extremely good-looking, to be terribly blasé and conceited and he kept flashing his eyes and teeth at me in a studied phoney manner which I could not stand. After a spell chez Regine's where all the men were greeted with kisses from Regine herself (another measure of success for the boys), we then went on to the Isle St. Louis, where people were dancing in the street beneath Chinese lanterns to a series of typical French accordion bands, and drinking wine whilst draped over or sitting on the wall overlooking the Seine. Here we ran into some film people, friends of theirs. We sat down at a table and ordered some drinks. There seemed to be some kind of Antonioni-type drama going on at which, not understanding French very well, I could only guess. But there was a lot of tearing off in fast sports cars, and a beautiful Swedish girl was sobbing into a glass of Pernod (I think it was) whilst a rather effeminate male sat there nodding moodily and not saying a word.

'What's going on?' I asked my Frenchman.

'Oh Ingrid is in love with Jean-Luc, but Jean-Luc is in love with Bertrand. Bertrand never speaks, he's a writer; and Ingrid threatens to kill herself if he continues to make Jean-Luc unhappy. But,' he added, 'don't you think they are amazingly beautiful people?'

Beautiful wouldn't have been exactly the adjective I should have chosen. Refugees from Pirandello's "Six Characters in Search Of An Author" would have been nearer the mark.

At one point my Frenchman excused himself from me to make a phone call. That was the last I saw of him. After a while I inquired of Guy de if he knew where 'himself' had gone.

'Oh, he's probably gone home,' he replied happily. 'He often does that!'

Presently I too drifted out of orbit of the rest of the party whilst dancing with a group of charming firemen. So after a while I decided to try to find my own way home alone. It wasn't easy, however, on such a night and after having drunk more than several glasses of wine. I finally danced, sang and staggered my way back to the apartment in time for breakfast with Henrietta and Fifi and a king-sized hangover.

Fifi was madly in love with the son of the Minister of the Interior, a very good-looking young intellectual, to whom she had been introduced by one of her co-mannequins. One night she arrived home with stars in her eyes and said that Alain had invited her to a grand reception at the *Petit Palais* where she would be presented to General de Gaulle.

'Just think Val,' she said, 'I keep saying over and over to myself: Felicity Wood from Margate!'

Henrietta usually went to bed at 9 o'clock, worn out by her own nervous energy. She had found her man and wasn't searching any further.

A few nights later, it chanced that we were all at home together for one evening. I had not had sight nor sound of my Frenchman since the storming of the Bastille. I had however had invitations from Fifi's Frenchman while Fifi was not home, at which I was more than a little surprised and saddened. It further transpired that Fifi had had invitations from my Frenchman. And then we discovered that Henrietta, meanwhile, had been propositioned right, left and centre by all our various escorts. All this proved to be quite a revelation to each of us and we wondered if this was the general custom in France. If so, we all agreed then it was a pretty sneaky way to carry on, and we held a council of war on the spot. We decided to show them that women are not always so thoroughly disloyal to their girl-friends where men are concerned, and that there is such a thing as honour amongst females as well as thieves. In contradiction to the popularly-held masculine viewpoint, women in fact can be very loyal friends. I am reminded of Kit.

Kit was American, a tough cookie from Chicago. She liked money and she liked to drink. She had an extremely slick elegant kind of chic which attracted Balmain.

One day after the show she and I called in at the Bellman Bar across the road for a *coup de champagne*. We were very thirsty after working hard in our hot-house all day. Boris the Russian Baron was sitting there, a large florid-faced gentleman with an expansive frame, a voice to match, and fierce-looking eyes. His head was sparsely populated with hair, and a large fold of flesh at the back of his neck gave sign of good living extended to excess. The fur hat and boots, enormous leather belt with ruby-studded buckle, and the gigantic cream silk shirt with a high collar embroidered with Russian flowers and symbols were all missing, and in actual fact Boris was dressed quite conventionally, but one nevertheless had the impression that this was what Boris was wearing. A flesh-and-blood residue from some Russian fantasy. He knew Kit already, and invited us both to share a bottle of champagne. Boris adored elegant women and kept saying that he had reached that age now when his intentions could only be interpreted as honourable. He liked very much to tease and to play jokes with a perfectly straight poker face until you flared up, whereupon he would let you down again with a delicate bump. At one point he made me so angry that I very nearly walked out, and he laughed in a great booming roar and called me a lioness. (I happened to be wearing a wig like a lioness at the time too.)

Boris was some kind of businessman. He travelled a lot, and had an American passport with extra pages added to it to carry all the stamps from exotic places such as most people only dream of. He was obviously very wealthy. He had no children but he did have an unofficially-adopted son whom he adored called Jonathan.

One night, shortly after I met him with Kit, Boris invited Kit and me to dine at one of the most excellent restaurants in Paris, La Perousse. He talked all the evening about Jonathan.

'You must meet Jonathan,' he kept repeating to me. 'He's English, very good-looking and very spoiled.'

'Look,' I said, 'I came to Paris to get away from Englishmen and on no account do I want to meet Jonathan. And besides,' I added for full measure, 'he sounds perfectly ghastly.'

The following day after the showing, a message came that someone wished to see me and was waiting in the downstairs salon. I clutched at my white overall and ran downstairs. There stood a very tall, fair, handsome young man with a basket in his arms, which he was holding somewhat gingerly.

'My name is Jonathan,' he said. 'Boris asked me to bring you this,' and he held out the basket to me. I peeped inside and gasped. It was a bear cub. The sweetest, softest, most cuddly, growly little thing you ever saw. Astonished? I was struck dumb and couldn't utter a word.

'Come and have some dinner with me tonight,' said

Jonathan. I nodded. 'Pick you up about eight then.' I nodded
dumbly again.

My Kinkajoo Honey-Bear, to give her full title, I named
Sophia, and we became tremendous friends though she was
rather a liability in a small apartment and was apt to sharpen
her claws on our carpet or on Felicity's bath towel. She would
also pee everywhere, with a special preference for the beds,
and once she got drunk on Henrietta's Martini. She demanded constant attention in fact, and was not exactly the most
practical of gifts. Her staple diet was bananas, which she held
in her hand and peeled delicately in a disconcertingly human
fashion. Her other passion was honey, and for the pursuit of
this delicacy nature had furnished her with a six-inch-long
tongue, for digging around in bees' nests no doubt. Sophia
however had an orifice complex, and any old orifice might
contain honey as far as she was concerned. Unsuspecting
guests would find a tongue pushed affectionately up their
nostrils or coming out of nowhere to explore the inside of an
ear, before we had had time to warn them. Her main
drawback, though, was the strange hours that she kept.
During the day she slept soundly until six o'clock in the
evening, and two tons of T.N.T. wouldn't have disturbed her.
At 6 p.m. she would yawn and open one eye, eat a banana
and jump down from her shelf in the kitchen with a thud. By
one o'clock in the morning she would be literally in full
swing, by which I mean leaping from the top of the
bathroom door to the top of the cistern, grabbing hold of
and swinging on the lavatory chain, and flushing the toilet all
night long.

One day a friend came round with a fox terrier. It was
love at first sight. They chased each other all over the
apartment, Sophia having the advantage in high places but
the terrier making up time on the flat. It seemed a pity to
break up such a beautiful relationship, so I let her go with
her true love and there she remains in the country, to this day.

Jonathan and I became good friends, however, and though we pursued different courses for different motives, we had certain things in common. He was twenty-five, an Old Etonian, ex-guards-officer from a noble family, who had never really done much except gamble and go to Deb parties. At least that's how I saw him. He was also well on the way to becoming the darling of Parisian society — they love English nobility in France. Boris was grooming him to succeed him in his business affairs, and also teaching him how to collect paintings and to appreciate the finer subtleties of life. It must have been a tremendous blow to Boris when Jonathan turned out eventually to be a rabid revolutionary and 'split', taking off with the New-York-based but wandering 'Living Theatre'.

The mannequins of Balmain are frequently invited to social events, including many film premières and first nights, in order to decorate the scene a little, and naturally we are always able to choose the most beautiful furs and dresses for the occasion. Once, whilst Jonathan was still my 'beau', we were all invited to a première and reception at the Moulin Rouge. The film was about a famous jewel robbery and we were invited to wear the fabulous jewels that appeared in the film. I chose to wear a simple white crêpe evening dress, with a full-length white ermine coat which was worth several thousand pounds. It was the perfect ensemble to show off the priceless *Collier de la Liberté*, a necklace of diamonds and emeralds that I was given to wear for the evening. I had invited Jonathan to escort me as besides other things he was well versed in this sort of evening, and even possessed a *smoking*, as the French call evening dress. All the other mannequins had invited suitably elegant escorts. Victoria had an Italian count, Danielle, a French 'de', and so on. The première was a huge success, or rather we were. Armed guards with machine guns, no less, followed us everywhere, and our photographs appeared in all the papers and on the T.V. plus various newsreels. After a sumptuous dinner and cabaret on the house at the Moulin Rouge, along with stars of the French movies, eight of us took off for Castel's. The scene there was a little different and the music infinitely better, though we were rather an unusual sight in our finery. We were shown to a table and Victoria immediately called for champagne. We danced up a storm until 5 a.m. My long white crêpe was beginning to look lived in, and at last we decided to call it a day, or rather a night. Imagine the scene therefore. There we were, the most richly-clad women in the world, escorted by the proverbial handsome young gentlemen with noble titles, but unfortunately little else; for when the bill came, none of us had a red cent between us. The proprietor suggested, politely I thought, that the men should leave their passports and that a few of us girls should leave our minks. Polite or not, we thought this a bit much and settled for the men's passports. When we came to leave, my escort, penniless and stripped even of his means of identification, helped me on with my multi-thousand-pound ermine, and we walked home.

All through an August heatwave, Hen, Fifi and I enjoyed life in our little attic. Paris became deserted because of the mass exodus of Parisians to the seaside. All of the shops and restaurants closed down, and often it was difficult to find a food shop open. We all had a hard time avoiding complications with husbands on the loose while wives were safely tucked away at Deauville or Juan-les-Pins — an occupational hazard in most cities during the month of August. Jonathan invited me to spend a few days at his parents' villa in Cadaques, in Spain. It seemed a good idea, so I arranged for a stand-in to take my place, and took a train and a bumpy local bus to the little fishing village on the Mediterranean.

Whenever I go to Spain, I seem to enter some dreamlike trance which stays with me until I leave. This was my first experience of this Fellini-esque world. Cadaques was full of pretty people. Rich hippies mostly, a mixture of American and English. A girl with long pale blonde hair, wearing a bikini, used to ride through the village bareback on a beautiful Palomino, looking like a goddess. How I envied her. Horses and sea. In the middle of the village square two Americans, one white with freaked-out hair and the other a negro, sat playing chess for days. Melina Mercouri and James Mason suddenly appeared with an entire film unit and re-enacted some kind of drama before my eyes, which added further to the luminous, dreamy, unreal atmosphere.

It was a marvellous relaxation after the sometimes harsh brittle glitter of Paris.

7

DAILY LIFE

It used to be a custom in Europe that when a young man from a wealthy upper-class family came of age he was taken to a famous couture house to watch the mannequin parade, in order to pick out for himself, not a dress, but a beautiful mannequin to have as his mistress and to keep suitably bestowed with presents of jewels, furs and carriages and maybe the odd racehorse or two. But never, of course, did he offer marriage. Such goings on, however, are comparatively rare nowadays. A few more years ago than one should mention one girl, a rather hard-featured ex-beauty, was reputed to have had the walls of her apartment in the Avenue George V papered with banknotes, a present from a wealthy South American with whom she had become acquainted. The legend also ran that once she had become angry with him for not making her an honest woman, and had refused to see him. Basically she just wanted what every woman wants, (with a whole lot more besides). Some days later a package arrived for her. Inside was a dish-mop — with a solid gold handle, custom-made by Cartier.

But most of the mannequins lead very normal lives and finish up by marrying very respectable doctors, lawyers, T.V. directors, insurance men and the like.

Once we had an American girl whose husband was reading for a law doctorate, while she was actually the breadwinner. But most mannequins do settle down eventually, after their short career, to married life and babies, unless their heads become so turned by the adulation they are used to receiving that they become impossible.

Some girls, on the other hand, become 'homosexual idols'. They are so brain-washed by certain designers and fashion photographers into believing in the extensions of elegance that some designers like to portray on women, that they forget what it is like to be a real woman. Many beautiful models are attracted by homosexuals because they appeal to their vanity and clothe them with superficial admiration. Garbo was a homosexual idol, in my opinion; I have never yet met a real man who liked her looks. So are Dietrich, Audrey Hepburn, and Dorothy Parker, though this latter is idolised for her bitchy wit and humour rather than her beauty. Women and men with a strong femine streak adore her, but not many *real* men. Real men prefer women such as Elizabeth Taylor who recently stated, 'Real men don't like skinny women – they only think they do because they are supposed to look better in clothes. But what happens when the clothes come off and you get between the sheets on a cold winter's night? Then they want something they know is a real woman'. Bravo Liz Taylor.

If a mannequin continues to look not more than twenty-four to twenty-five until she is well into her thirties, then she can without any difficulty extend her modelling career for quite a long while. There is never really any set age-limit for retirement. It depends upon the style, elegance and grace of the woman. A photographic model, on the other hand, can become 'over exposed', which means that her face has been used in so many ads that people have grown tired of it. This can cause a photographic model to retire at the ripe old age of twenty-one – having of course made her fortune by then, though I don't suppose that anyone gives her a gold watch!

Personally I have often resolved not to continue modelling after the age of thirty. Competition is strong, and new, fresh

beauties are coming up all the time. I would hate to be an
'old model'. The modelling game offers many things to a girl,
money for some and travel; but chiefly, I suppose, an escape
from one's environment. Most girls profit by this escape, one
way or another, and all kinds of doors open to a model girl.

One day when I arrived in the *cabine*, I sensed an air of
excitement around. Somebody had heard it rumoured that
we were going on a trip. Sure enough, later that day a notice
was pinned up advising us of a trip to Stockholm to present
the collection before the Swedish Royal Family. The day
started with a rendezvous at 6 a.m. at Orly where, in spite of
the hour, a full *couture* send-off took place, with a bevy of
photographers and bouquets for everyone. We must have
been an elegant sight for our sleepy fellow-travellers as we
boarded the plane. At Stockholm there were more bouquets
of typically Swedish flowers, and more photographers as we
stepped from our plane into the waiting cars which then
drove us to the Grand Hotel. Balmain had the best suite
reserved for himself and the most elegant rooms for us.
Already there were presents of perfume, make-up, L.P's and
more flowers to welcome us.

The presentation was to be in the very elegant all-golden
City Hall, which I could see from the balcony of my room.
After a short rest we were driven to the palatial surroundings.
A great stone and mosaic ante-room served as a dressing-
room, giving on to a majestic stone staircase which swept
down to the catwalk. It appeared to be at the very least the
length of Southend Pier. Rows upon rows of plush chairs
with a throne in the place of honour for the Prince Bertil and
the members of the Royal Family. King Gustav was over
eighty and was not really disposed to fashion shows, and so
was represented by the prince. When we tried out the route,
we discovered that on leaving the catwalk we had to ascend by
a back staircase to the upper floor, and then run like crazy
through room after room, skating across polished floors, in

order to be on time for the next change.

The evening came, and the ex-palace was all glittery-gold with hundreds of real candles burning in the candelabra, and flaming torches marking the entrance. Millions of flowers were banked up the staircase and a full orchestra played in the minstrel's gallery. The spectacle began.

Everyone found their way back to the dressing-room except Christine, who got lost without her spectacles on and missed five of her turns while she fumbled around in the west wing somewhere. Standing waiting our turn on the balcony, we were able to watch each other's progress along the catwalk. It was fascinating to observe the other mannequins presenting themselves, and to study the different styles of walking. Tania walked like an articulated truck, bent in the middle; her lower half seeming to be entirely independent of her upper half. Naomi also had a pelvic walk; she 'climbed' along the catwalk with her bottom tucked between her knees as though her suspenders were attached to her ankle socks. Very effective. Victoria did her famous wild-cat act, hurling herself from one end of the catwalk to the other at the speed of light, glaring balefully at the audience and making them twitch nervously. One girl looked as though she would fall over backwards any minute and another walked the length of the catwalk with her arms outstretched sideways. Rosemary stalked along with her arms firmly glued to her sides, reminding me rather of an ostrich.

One can afford to be a little extravagant during a big show like this. Naomi was so meticulous about her performance and appearance that she used to stand holding her hands up in the air just before she made her entrance so that they would appear nice and white with no veins showing. Many mannequins develop a backward-leaning walk, so as not to break the line of the dress when taking a step forward; a good mannequin, indeed, would rather break her neck. One Dutch mannequin walked bolt upright, moving only her feet in tiny steps; in an evening dress she looked as though she were being pushed along on a stand. Balmain fired her on the spot in a fit of pique; but I heard later she was very soon snapped up by Dior.

I would love to see how I walk myself. People tell me I have great aplomb, whatever that means, and Eric once paid me a wonderful compliment by telling someone (in front of me) that I have that magnetism that commands people to take notice when I am showing a dress. I wish this applied when I speak. Generally, when I open my mouth people take it as a signal all to talk at the same time. I seem to be a sort of verbal starter-pistol. Well, why not; we all have interesting things to tell.

But anyway I certainly commanded attention during my debut before the Swedish Royal Family. It will be memorable for one thing if nothing else, for when I came on in my final evening dress, all-gold and mediaeval-style, with a very low-cut square neck and long sleeves, heavily jewel-encrusted, I tripped on the stairway and made the last ten steps on my behind. A gasp came from the audience, I calmly disentangled my heel from the hem of my dress, and drawing myself up with whatever dignity I could muster, I shot them a withering glance, stuck my shoe back on again, and took off arrogantly along the catwalk amid rousing applause. I was shaken and bruised, but the show must go on.

In spite of the various crises and panics behind the scenes the show was a tremendous success, and afterwards a formal dinner was laid on for us. It turned out to be a hilarious affair when Balmain managed to cut through the traditional Scandinavian ice by telling slightly *risqué* after-dinner stories in his perfect English.

Later still we took a nightclub by storm. Balmain, who loves to dance, was kept busy with eight partners, although we were also besieged with invitations from many handsome Swedes. Victoria had been sampling the schnapps, and danced so much that she finally threw her shoes off. At one point she came back to our table, put her feet up, and exhibited her stockings hanging in tatters with no feet left in them.

'Oh do look at your stockings,' exclaimed Naomi, shocked to the core.

Victoria promptly dragged her long scarlet nails down each of Naomi's elegant legs, ripping hers to shreds also.

'Now,' she cried, 'just look at yours.'

It takes all sorts to make a world, as Victoria would be the first to admit.

Dana, the forlorn countess, was rather a strange girl. I knew her slightly from fashion shows when we had worked together. Shortly after our return from the Swedish trip, she turned up one day at Balmain's and greeted me like a long-lost sister. 'My husband has left me,' she shrieked from one end of the salon to the other. 'I have to find a job,' she almost sobbed. All the *vendeuses* and a few of the customers poked their heads out of their fitting-rooms to see what all the commotion was about. 'Please, you have to help me,' she pleaded to me.

Well it just so happened that they needed another mannequin in the *cabine* since the Dutch girl had been so unceremoniously dismissed, so she was quickly taken on. I think the title helped a bit. She was also rather beautiful. She was very grateful and seemed to consider me her saviour. 'Let me invite you to dinner,' she said. I had nothing to do that evening, so I agreed to go along as she seemed lonely.

We dined at a bar-cum-restaurant-nightclub. There were not many people there, and Dana explained that it was early, and the place generally filled up after the theatre. There was a bar near the entrance and a small dance-floor in the middle. Presently a creature all dressed in black shiny plastic swished in and greeted everyone effusively.

A last-minute conference

On board the cruise-ship—wearing a sheet!

'That's ....', (the proprietor) whispered Dana.

'Him or her?' I enquired.

'A.C./D.C,' she replied.

Then Dana went on to pour out her troubles. She had eventually married a very wealthy Frenchman, and her greatest ambition was to be a rich widow. The count, needless to say, had thrown her out. I began to see why, poor man.

Presently the place filled up, and I began to notice something strange. Apart from the barman, there were no men in the place. A few couples were dancing, but they were all girls. Many were wearing dark glasses, a few wore trousers and most were very pretty.

'Dance with me, Valerie,' said Dana.

'Not likely,' I replied vehemently.

I never could stand to see two women dancing together, even in Billericay, at the local Old-Time hop. When Dana went to powder her nose and left me alone at the table, a sloe-eyed beauty sidled up and invited me to dance with her. I was a little stunned, and trying desperately to remain cool I stammered that I was already with someone. She retreated, but just then a young man with a bandage around his ear, looking like Van Gogh, came over to me, bowed, and invited me to dance. In desperation I agreed. He spoke good English.

'I just stopped by to see my friend the barman, and we have a bet on,' he said. 'We bet that you, he and I were the only normal people in the place.'

'Oh really,' I replied, still mystified.

'Yes,' he said. 'What's a nice girl like you doing in a Dyke bar?'

At this point I noticed an air of growing hostility in the atmosphere. Couples of girls dancing cheek to cheek would sidle up close, lower their dark glasses and peer at me with a mixture of scorn and spite. After a few rounds of the floor, I decided to 'split'. Dana, I resolved, could well look after herself and must be familiar with the scene.

'May I escort you,' demanded Van Gogh.

'No I don't think so. Thanks all the same. But you could find me a taxi, please.' I got my coat and made a rapid exit.

'By the way, what happened to your ear?' I asked him as I stepped into the taxi.

'I cut it off,' he grinned back amiably. I sank back into the reassuring security of the taxi and fled off into the night. Personally I am of the opinion that Adam and Eve had the best idea yet.

Van Gogh freaks apart, and in spite of various influences to the contrary, I remain firmly attracted to the balance of opposites. Magnetism between North and North tends to lack an exciting natural phenomenon. Likewise, I feel that the Women's Lib. Movement is striving to condemn us to the same mass mediocrity now enjoyed by modern man, rather than to extend that special freedom to be illogical in a feminine way and to be, as individuals, outside the indoctrinated mass. If women do have a very special function in this modern world, it is to preserve that last fundamental vestige of difference, a rock without which we would all be swept into the same mundane non-identifiable facelessness. Let's get the women out of the factories and into a different sort of freedom. To convert the slaves into Roman soldiers is not at all my idea of liberty.

Meanwhile, back at the salon, the private customers were busy doing their shopping at this time. The show was held up one day for three-quarters of an hour by the royal prerogative of Queen Fabiola, no less, and her lady-in-waiting. This delay provided us, amongst other things, with time in which to practice our curtseys. The queen was in fact charming and really quite ordinary, to look at, graciously smiling at all and sundry and not even wearing a crown. Felicity would have been even more impressed than she had been when she was to be presented to General de Gaulle, for truly there is no substitute in the European mind, in terms of pomp and grandeur, for genuine royalty.

In terms of grandeur of another sort, I recall once being asked to show a long, slinky, off one shoulder, wine velvet dress in one of the fitting rooms. The customer was the most enormous, grey-haired lady from Texas with an ample bosom, who looked a little like ex-President Johnson and was possessed of a very grand though somewhat iron personality. She had on a copy of 'my' dress, and kept wielding a long solid-gold cigarette holder dangerously close to my eye as she peered at the seams on the prototype. I stood patiently while she muttered to her designated *vendeuse* in a gravel voice. Then looking up I noticed a whole bunch of Arab workmen in the street outside, grinning and cavorting around their shovels in grotesque imitation of the scene before them. I couldn't help seeing their point of view. Imitations beget imitations. Though I have no doubt that as far as my Texas 'empress' was concerned, her grandeur sprang from an oil well and not from back numbers of Queen magazine.

Another time I had to show a lovely little white tailored afternoon dress to a customer. I swept into the fitting room, stopped, and looked around. The room appeared at first to be empty, and then I heard a faint croak from the direction of a heap of clothes on a chair. Suddenly I saw her. A poor little old lady, she couldn't have been a day under ninety, was sitting there in her sagging lace underwear, commanding me imperiously to 'come a little closer, dear.' She wasn't much more than a skeleton, and her bony fingers were emblazoned with diamond rings. Around her throat was a choker of pearls and rubies and there were two great smears of rouge on her parchment cheeks. At first I felt saddened by the obvious contrast in our appearances – and then later I thought how enchanting that this little old witch should still have the strength and desire to be *coquette* at her age.

A whole host of well-known show biz people and film stars shop at Balmain, not to mention real life stars too. Madame Batista, wife of the ex-dictator of Cuba, for instance. She speaks only Spanish, and regularly buys her entire wardrobe from Balmain, using an interpreter. Grace Kelly came one day to the show and bought three evening dresses; Ingrid Bergman, my favourite actress, is also quite a regular customer, mainly for evening dresses, at which Balmain excels. Marlene Dietrich bought a sumptuous black diamond mink coat and had endless fittings before it was good enough to pass her meticulous requirements. Sammy Davis Junior appeared one day and just for a laugh gave us an impromptu demonstration of the 'model's walk'. One woman always views the collection with her husband. They are both tiny in stature. She dresses like a fifty-year-old version of Shirley Temple and her husband, who had reputedly made a fortune selling aeroplanes to the Africans, looks like a miniature Rudolph Valentino with pointed, two-tone shoes, long greasy curls, and diamond and ruby rings on his languid fingers. Their grey poodle has to have a similar outfit to that of Madame, and even turned up one day in his own mink coat and with genuine rubies studding his collar.

After Stockholm we were invited to London where Princess Margaret had requested a Royal Show (or perhaps commanded is the regal word). It was a strange feeling to visit my native land as a foreigner, for I was looked upon as being a Parisienne.

'Your English is excellent,' said Billy Wallace to me at a dinner party he and his charming wife gave for us.

'I was educated in England,' I replied truthfully.

Even more astonished was the young man placed next to me at dinner. During the shrimp cocktail, I turned to him and drawled in my most 'blah' accent, 'I suppose you went to Eton, then had a spell in the Hussars, and now you are something in advertising.'

'Good heavens. How on earth did you know all that?' he spluttered. Apparently I even had the correct regiment.

There must have been at least fifty photographers following us everywhere we went, and we were escorted around by the most elegant 'hons' and 'sirs'. It was fun to be treated like visiting royalty. The presentation took place in the beautiful, though oddly named, Fishmongers Hall in the City of London. Princess Margaret and Tony Armstrong-Jones were both looking tanned, healthy, and glamorous, having just returned from a trip to the West Indies. Once again we were obliged to curtsey before their Royal Highnesses, whilst presenting our first dresses. They were seated halfway down the catwalk, and were not to difficult to pick out for anyone with normal vision. However myopic Christine, alas, mistook one of the ushers standing beside a bust of Queen Victoria for the Royal couple and dropped him the most fabulous curtsey. It was all right though. Princess Margaret smiled and Tony either winked or had a sudden nervous twitch and everything continued without interruption. We never did have the heart to tell Christine.

Naturally my family were invited to the show and they were proud and delighted to see their daughter in such company, though my father was a little taken aback by my new chic appearance. 'I liked you better in pigtails,' he muttered.

The phone rang for me one day after the show and a stranger introduced himself and said: 'We met at a reception at the Palace in Stockholm. Do you remember?'

I didn't remember at all in fact, as I had met so many people at that reception, but when he invited me to dine I agreed out of curiosity. A meeting-place was arranged in the Bar Anglais of the Plaza Athenée on the Avenue Montaigne in Paris. The bar was full when I arrived, and not knowing who to look for I asked to be shown to a table by myself, never doubting that he would recognise *me*. Three cigarettes and two martinis later the bar had almost emptied except for a couple of American fashion buyers and a few other stragglers, including a rather foreign-looking man. Just when I was on the point of leaving the man, who had been sitting at the next table since my arrival, stood up and bowing his tall frame presented his card.

'Excuse me,' he said, 'I have been observing you. You must be Valerie, but you do not look the same as I remember.' Of course. He remembered me covered in chinchilla and diamonds leaning on the Rolls Bentley, for he was its owner.

'Oh really? It must be the lighting,' I answered.

After some preliminaries, we went to dine at Taillevant. Over the caviar, he recounted to me his history and lamented sadly the changing of the Paris scene. It had not been like this in his day. He had known the real Paris, when groups of rich young bloods raced around in fast sports cars, kidnapping beautiful girls and spending fortunes on champagne and roses, beautiful clothes and elegant dinners, plus the occasional seemingly inevitable duel. Times had changed, and it wasn't the same anymore. To my consternation, I noticed tears tolling down his cheeks. Good heavens! What on earth should I do? I thought. I never could stand scenes in public, Change the subject quickly.

'Do you believe in ghosts?' I asked — the first thing that came into my head. What a mistake!

'It is strange that you should say that,' he replied with a queer look in his eye. 'I believe that I am the reincarnation of the Emperor Franz Joseph of Austria.' He spoke with a kind of quiet conviction. 'When I saw you waiting there tonight I wished to observe you to see if you had the manner and breeding of an Empress, and I find indeed that you do.'

'Have another drink, Prince,' I suggested. I've always been a sucker for nut cases. This one definitely had a problem. Distinct schizoid tendency with delusions of grandeur, paranoia, etc. Two glasses of Château Lafitte Rothschild later, he was recounting to me stories of his beautiful mother, with tears streaming and sobs reverberating through the restaurant. The waiters were very discreet, in fact I think he was one of their well-known 'characters'.

'There, there,' I consoled him, as they presented him with a phenomenal bill and we all helped him into a taxi. 'It will all be better in the morning,' I assured him as I bade him farewell and then rushed home to tell all to Hen and Fifi.

During a gala night dinner at the restaurant Lasserre I was 'discovered' by a very wealthy French industrialist. He wangled an introduction through a mutual acquaintance and invited me out one evening. 'There will be four of us and we can all meet at my apartment,' he said.

The penthouse was of Louis XV elegance, with small tables laden with various *objets d'art* and exquisite polished stone eggs and things, and an incredible view of the Arc de Triomphe. Monsieur was charmingly and alarmingly frank.

'I am forty-two and I have been married for twenty years. My children are grown up and my wife and I go our separate ways. Soon I will divorce, when I meet someone younger; I am very wealthy and successful, but one thing is missing.' He continued, 'I need a beautiful, elegant young wife to be a hostess and to help me to entertain my friends.'

What a transaction, I thought to myself.

The other couple consisted of a man, about the same age as my industrialist friend, and a very pretty and elegant woman in her late twenties, dressed in white fox. As we left for dinner and were walking to the cars, my 'monsieur' asked me, 'Which car would you like to go in? There is this one,' he indicated a sleek black Citroën, 'or this one', a Lancia Sport, 'or this one I use for traffic', a Mini Cooper, 'or the Jaguar'. We finally settled for the Jaguar. At dinner the conversation drifted around to Deauville. I had never been there as it usually means staying overnight, and the type of man who usually invites one there is not the kind with whom one wishes to stay overnight.

'We can fly there for the day in my private plane,' said my monsieur with instant propriety. But to say that our relationship lacked romance would be to say the very least. Presently we fell to talking about other people, and he told me how clever and intelligent he thought the other woman in our party was. She had 'come from nothing', but had become the mistress of his friend, who was also married with three kids. They had been together for ten years, and now she had her own boutique. There, now, wasn't that a good success story for you?

Well, I could not really see what was so great about that and said so. After that the relationship shrivelled completely and we ended up in total silence. Moral: beware of wealthy forty-year-old Frenchmen. They are all charming, they are all married, and they practically all have mistresses; and not merely the wealthy ones either. In England and the States marriage is generally regarded as the end of a gad-about flighty life of pick-ups and one-night stands. In France the marriage certificate is usually regarded as a licence to commence fornication. (Prior to marriage they seem to prefer the company of books or other boys.)

It was during the month of March that we were invited by U.T.A. Airline to present the Summer Collection in Lagos, Nigeria. We left Paris very early on a Saturday morning, bundled up in furs as it was snowing. Six hours later we touched down in Lagos in hair-bedraggling heat. A whole tribe of Africans with grass skirts, beads, feathers, and bones through their nostrils charged towards us with spears carried low and animal-skin shields held high. They stopped dead as they reached us, fortunately, and then peered at us curiously. If we thought they were extraordinary, they thought us even more so, and in fact as I looked around at us, they had a point too; thin, anaemic, and colourless we appeared by contrast. All the way from the plane to the reception building they escorted us with dances and chants, one man walking on stilts and another turning somersaults. At the reception, a group of bossy colonial Englishwomen 'took charge' and 'exhibited' some native women exhibiting African arts and crafts. After shaking hands and being photographed with all the *Obas* (the tribal chiefs) who were very venerable, dignified gentlemen who just adored being photographed, we piled into official cars and took off through the jungle for Lagos. Banks of exotic flowers and flocks of strange birds in incredible colours provided a feast for our eyes. The motorcycle escort sat on their sirens for most of the twenty miles or so, and one poor black man was so overjoyed to see us (or so we were led to believe) that he prostrated himself in the middle of the road, shouting hysterically, until the police very roughly and unceremoniously scooped him up and locked him away.

The Hotel Ikuyu was, by contrast to the picturesque squalor of the outskirts of Lagos, shining white and very modern. Drama was added by the fact that a Nigerian president had been shot dead on the steps of this hotel the previous week. A note was waiting for me at the hotel reception desk. It was from a photographer in London with whom I had worked at one time, asking me to meet him for cocktails on the terrace at six o'clock. It was so nice to meet someone I knew in such a strange place. Not that we lacked escorts, as we later found out, for it seemed that suddenly business was booming at the hotel. At the news of our arrival, every light-skinned bachelor for miles around had headed for the Hotel Ikuyu and checked in for the weekend, and those who couldn't get a room were jockeying for position in the bars and patios. It seems that the only women in Nigeria are either married, black or missionaries. My photographer had a hard time getting through the throng.

For the rest of the day we lazed around at the pool and rested in our air-conditioned rooms. In the evening a reception was held in our honour at the elegant home of the French Ambassador. Here once again were all the tribal chieftains dressed in gloriously brilliant coloured robes, with their so tall and elegant wives wearing enormous turbans wound elaborately around their heads. The gardens were hung with Chinese lanterns and white-coated house-boys darted everywhere balancing tiny gold trays of champagne. One of the *Obas* told me gleefully that Paris was his favourite city. He went there once a year for a weekend, taking in the Folies Bergère, then the Lido, and afterwards Pigalle. Then he caught the plane home again! It was his annual event. The evening finished up in the usual fashion of our trips abroad, in a discotheque, but this time it was in order to cool off. The air-conditioning was indeed icy and a welcome relief.

The following day a trip to the beach and a picnic had been arranged for us. We set off early before the sun had reached its zenith, with strict orders from Balmain and Eric *not* to get brown or we would all be fired. But they underestimated the fierce African sun, which needed no more than three minutes to cook one right through, flash heat style. Victoria was determined to remain pale, and wore a long-sleeved turquoise-blue silk Balmain dress with a large-brimmed matching hat and sunglasses, stockings and high heels. Lina was also dressed to kill with a hair piece, false eyelashes and all her jewellery. Tania caused a sensation in a see-through blouse, being naked as a babe underneath. The rest of us discarded shoes and stockings and went native. After a boat trip across the bay we landed on the edge of a jungle and then went on a minor safari to the beach, passing all kinds of pitiful beggars and lepers and snake charmers on the way, eager for our attention; droves of small boys padded along beside us, grinning and holding out their hands.

At the beach we all crowded into the shade of a mud hut,

remembering Balmain's warning, but it was too late for most of us and my nose had already begun to peel. Maggie and Edith had forgotten their swimming costumes, so ended up in bras and pantie girdles. Victoria at last took off her hat and lay down in a corner of the hut. The charming English couple who escorted us produced (much to the disgust of the French palate) warm beer and cucumber sandwiches, after which the rest of us donned our bikinis and took to the waves. By one-thirty it was so hot that even Lina ventured to descend to the water, wearing a towel draped elegantly, Grecian-style. She also had forgotten to bring a bikini and with her jewels and hair she looked like the Queen of Sheba annointing herself in the River Jordan. Balmain, who had followed our tracks and arrived later, also provided a rare sight as he eventually dived in with a piece of native material girding his loins sarong style. Unfortunately, as soon as it became wet, the material also became transparent! Eric sat in the shelter of the hut with Victoria and groaned and muttered about how terrible we all looked.

Back at the hotel Tania found a lizard in her room and promptly passed out, and Victoria took a shower with her eyelashes on and watched them disappear down the plug-hole amid wails of anguish, while some of us sneaked out to the street market in search of souvenirs. In the market I met a travelling witch-doctor. He was wearing a tiger's mane around his waist and tiger's teeth hung from his ears and round his neck. Smears of purple and white paint decorated his chest and face, and he sat still as a waxwork blinking like a cat in the sun before a tray of charms and potions to keep away the evil spirits. As I was bending to examine a beautiful necklace, he said in a strong American accent, 'You don't need my ju-ju's lady, you got shining ways. How about a book of my poetry instead. One dollar.'

He fished in the bundle that held his belongings and produced a book of poetry with the name Ted Jones on the cover. The title was *The Head Shrinker*. I thanked him and read a little. It was what he would have called 'a gas'; really fine poetry, very sensitive, yet strong and full of happiness. I bought the book and, taking the Nigerian equivalent of one dollar, he said, 'Now, would you like to come and help me celebrate the sale of a book of my poetry? You've just stirred an old fire. I'd sort of abandoned it – the writing of poetry, I mean. I've been living my 'thing'. I make a bit on the tourists when I'm in town, but I don't need much. I dig my thing. It's nice. I call it my Ju-Ju thing.'

We made our way through the busy market-place to the other end where we sat around with a jumble of other people and drank a delicious drink from the coconut shell. Ted seemed to be known for many Nigerians smiled at him as we passed. He was clearly a 'character'. He told me that he had originally come from Fort Wayne, Indiana, but that after a life of wandering he had settled on an ancestral home. He had been married to a Swedish girl but she hadn't been able to adapt and had long since gone home. He was still wandering, but here for some reason he was well received wherever he went, and he stayed a few days here and there just 'doing his thing' as he called it. He had picked up an astonishing amount of tribal lore and claimed that he could cure people of bad spirits by 'feeling them with his eyes'. He had the whole thing worked out, including various herbal potions and poultices, and a little Chinese acupuncture that he had once picked up in Algeria. The Chinese had apparently set up numerous acupuncture clinics as part of a Chinese medical aid scheme and he had followed their mysterious doings with his usual avid interest in his surroundings. The only thing he was really adamant about was that he didn't want to leave Africa. He felt useful and he'd found a sort of peace within himself. I could see this in his face; he looked radiant. I wanted to invite him back to the hotel so that I could show off my find to my friends but he declined and thanking me went away, leaving me among the Negroes. I saw his point and made my way back to the hotel alone. His was the real Africa.

Before we began our show there was a fashion parade of Nigerian fashions with Nigerian mannequins. Ted Jones would have been fascinated, irrespective of his ideals. The mannequins were tall, proud girls. Their beauty, however, was marred by one strange incongruity: they all wore platinum-blonde Marilyn Monroe-type wigs.

Their full-dress native clothes were sensational, with a wonderful use of imagination and a completely new angle on fashion. Naturally so, I suppose, since the influences on their trends have such utterly different origins.

Our own sunburn had become quite fiery in the interim, but not half as fiery as Eric's temper when he saw us. 'You don't look chic at all,' he said to me cuttingly as I frantically applied more pale green powder to my nose. Even Victoria hadn't escaped. The sun had cast a ray through a crack in the wall of the mud hut and dealt her a cruel blow across the back, and Balmain's witty commentary was spiced with words such as *langouste* (lobster) and *crevette* (shrimp). The audience loved us though, and were thoroughly entertained. Our clothes looked ravishingly sophisticated and intricate in comparison with the gaudy simplicity of the African colours.

My photographer friend, who was down there taking pictures for a calendar, met me afterwards and a whole crowd of us went on a tour of local night spots; native Ted Jones ones, not the smart glossy ones where one might just as well be anywhere else in the world. We danced the *Meringué* to some incredibly distorted sounds piped through an ancient speaker system, and watched an African pick up a bicycle in his front teeth, and much much later we watched the dawn come up from the veranda of somebody's villa. Our plane left at 10 o'clock and we had a prior rendezvous at 8 a.m. so it didn't seem worth going to bed for one hour. I decided to sustain myself on yet more champagne, so as not to miss a moment of this strange and beautiful country — not to mention the excellent champagne. By the time we had reached the airport, and before boarding the plane, I was feeling a little — shall we say — under the weather. The flight was delayed for an hour, so after a while I crept off to a secluded spot to nurse my maxi hangover in the shade of an strange exotic-looking tree. Once there, I noticed that there were, hanging within the tree, several elongated birds nests. I lay down and gazed up through the branches at the clear blue sky. Well, not quite clear, for presently I noticed a large dark bird hovering overhead. It seemed to be almost suspended in the hot air. Suddenly I realised to my horror that it was a vulture. It must have taken one look at my carcass and thought, 'Ah Hum, this one's obviously on it's last knockings, I think I'll stick around!' The way I felt, the bird's opinion wasn't far from the truth, so I picked a colony of ants out of my Roger Vivier shoes and limped back to the relative security of the airport bar.

8

UPS AND DOWNS

A few weeks after our return from Africa, I was asked to do a hair show. A hair show is a lucrative thing to do occasionally. They usually pay well, and some of the top Parisian hairdressers travel all over the world giving demonstrations with three or four model girls in tow. But one has to be prepared to put up with sitting for hours under hot lights, under the gaze of a somewhat noisy rabble, while some self-important twit messes around with your crowning glory. It's rather like a public execution.

I have the sort of hair that sends hairdressers into ecstasy because it is very thick and always does what it is told to do. Every time I go to a new hairdresser I see him getting glassy-eyed, and the next thing I know he's asking me to do a show with him. I've had offers to go to such far-off places as Rio de Janiero and Tokyo, but of course I have always had to turn these down since it would mean leaving Balmain for a week or two and they wouldn't be very happy about that. Sometimes, however, these gigs take place at weekends when we are free. Such was the present case, and I was booked by a well-known Parisian coiffeur to do a show for him in Milan. We left on a Friday night, three models and two crimpers.

I knew I was in Italy the minute we stepped off the plane, as the customs man insisted upon searching our bags with one hand and nonchalantly patting me on the bottom with the other, without even looking. I feel sorry for Italian men really. They all seem so lonely and frustrated, and they make life unbearable for women. I mean, if you ever want to be alone and independent you just don't have a chance in Italy.

The show was held in a vast Exhibition Hall and was for mea sheer nightmare. Italians are known to be volatile, and here they were all wired for sound and amplified into the bargain. There was a stage upon which about three hairdressers simultaneously performed their tricks, creating fantastic styles in three minutes flat, starting from the roller stage and finishing amid a cloud of hair laquer and a burst of applause from the 30,000 gawping spectators. When my turn came I sat perspiring under the hot lights, my ears numb from the noise, and feeling distinctly twitchy about the row of instruments of torture that my crimper was setting out upon his tray. 'I just want to cut a leetle whisker,' he said through a tightly clenched, sadistic smile. It was useless to protest. I finished up with one side of my hair about two inches longer than the other, and four things the size of an orange made of real hair dangling around my ears. When I was shown the mirror I felt, and I am sure I looked, just like a despondant beagle.

If someone were to offer you the chance to go on a two-week Mediterranean cruise, taking in Cannes, Athens, the Greek Islands, Beirut and Istanbul, with a wardrobe of clothes by Balmain, shoes by Roger Vivier (minus the ants) and wigs by Alexandre, plus all expenses and a salary on top, you would surely find it hard to believe it possible. But that is just what happened to me next.

It was the month of May when I found myself representing the House of Balmain along with eleven other mannequins, one from each of the *couture* houses, aboard a luxury-cruise liner. The cruise was being organised by the International Silk Association. It was a floating mobile convention, with representatives present from all over the world, including the United States and of course Japan.

Above. At the Athens Hilton, wearing a ravishing navy and yellow
organza
Below. On the cat-walk at the Hotel Phoenecia at Beirut, built over a
swimming-pool. The evening dress and coat are pink and white zibeline

Bronze and gold sequin-encrusted ball-gown and coat by Balmain.
Hair by Alexandre

Upon a sea as calm as the proverbial mill pond we set off
from the Bay of Cannes for Athens and our first port of call.
There followed two glorious days of lounging around the
swimming pool making small talk and sipping long cool
drinks. We played deck tennis and admired the beautiful
ocean. It was bliss. There was only one fly in the ointment,
and that was a woman of aristocratic family who was the
'Majordomo' of the mannequins. She was what people would
describe as an aging beauty, and with her slanting cat's eyes
she had once been a mannequin, which perhaps had
something to do with her reaction towards me. Her attitude
appeared to be one of sheer, undistilled animosity. From
Notorious Parisienne Covergirl to cantankerous eye-
scratching jealousy. Boy, did she make me nervous! The more
nervous I became the more I did the wrong thing, and by half
way through the trip we were in a state of total war.

It should have been such a beautiful cruise but it was
completely ruined for me, and when I come to write about it
I can only think about that woman. She always seemed to be
on my back – perhaps because I gave an impression of being
too relaxed and carefree about my job. Uninitiated or
non-professional people might think that I am not quite
organised enough or am too vague to know what I am
doing. In fact, since I know I have this reputation for
vagueness I always make a special effort to see that I have *all*
my shoes, gloves, jewellery, hair pieces, etc. just so. Therefore, just before the opening of the show at the Athens
Hilton, while everyone else was off having supper before the
show, I was in the *cabine* carefully checking off all my items
when to my horror I discovered that the pink sharkskin shoes
that went with my final ensemble were missing. I turned the
whole place upside down searching for them and checked and
rechecked my shoe boxes as well as everyone elses, but they
were nowhere to be found. They must have been lost in
transit I concluded with a sinking feeling, and I prepared to
raise the alarm. I went along to the dining-room, marched up

to her ladyship, and announced dramatically that my pink shoes were nowhere to be found and that they must either have been stolen or lost in transit. *'Mais ce n'est pas possible,'* she screamed. 'How can you be so careless!' I hated her for her scepticism and refusal to believe what seemed to be an evident truth. The expensive shoes were not there, and I certainly had not eaten them as an *hors d'oeuvre*. I attempted to explain this to her, but lost my cool. We concluded the imparting of my bit of news with a toe to toe slanging match, all of which did nothing to improve our previously bad relations.

When I finally stomped back to the *cabine* white with rage, slammed the door, lit a cigarette, tapping my foot to cool off, I noticed peaking furtively from a corner a pair of pink sharkskin shoes. I would have gone back and apologised, but I reckoned that the woman had merited the angry disdain I had heaped upon her, in view of her intolerable refusal even to conceive that my story *might* have been true.

In Beirut we found ourselves sitting next to one another one night in a night club to which we had both been invited by a very charming, wealthy, and cosmopolitan mutual friend. I was seated on a banquette between them, making polite conversation with our host. It was difficult to hear conversation above the noise of the band. As the evening wore on, I became aware of the baroness nudging me in the ribs and saying (as I thought), 'How long does this place stay open till?' So I replied gaily, 'Oh just until dawn I expect!'.

Her face turned white with rage and her lips curled in an ugly sneer as I smiled at her. Suddenly I realised, in retrospect and with a shock, that in fact she had said, 'How much longer are you going to monopolize monsieur in conversation?' Poor woman; I suddenly felt very sorry for her. I really hadn't meant to upset her, so I made my exit.

During the show at the Istanbul Hilton, she had her revenge by 'corpsing' me on the catwalk. There I was, dedicated to my task of showing an exquisite evening dress to 700 exotic internationals, when I spun around to face the entrance and had a glimpse of a ghastly face, enveloped in a look of horror, mouthing frantic things at me through the curtain. The audience of course couldn't see her; but I was panic-stricken, wondering what I could be doing wrong. Trying not to show any sign, I continued to show off the dress and then made my exit. This was greeted by a crescendo of screams from her. Apparently a pretty lace bra had somehow or other become hooked into the hem of my dress, and I had trailed it all around the catwalk with me. Talk about a jinx. She only had to look at me and I would do something wrong.

By the time we came to the end of our cruise I had begun to feel as though we were aboard the Titanic. I'm sure I would have hit that iceberg twice a night and three times on matinées. Such petty nonsense is, thank God, fairly infrequent; however it does crop up now and then even so. Worse than politicians.

A few months later at the beginning of September I had the chance of another cruise which, for obvious reasons, I turned down. Pierre Balmain, however, prevailed upon me to come along, and stressed that this cruise would complete my recovery from the previous one. This time each mannequin had only four dresses to show, and as I had the most spectacularly beautiful evening dress the honour of showing last fell to me. My dress was of pale pink and white silk Ziberline, the bodice and hemline encrusted with pearls and diamonds. Over this was a full-length evening coat of the same material, in white lined with pink, which billowed out behind me as I walked and enabled me to make some spectacular spins and flourishes on the podium. However in Beirut I was forced to minimise the pirouettes for safety's sake, as the catwalk, although in a sumptuous setting on the elegant terrace of the Hotel Phoenicia overlooking the Mediterranean, was constructed over a *swimming pool*. Now one of my worst nightmares has always been that I should over-balance and fall off the catwalk, so when I saw this setting I vowed not to touch one tiniest sip of anything alcoholic until after the snow, and then sent off a postcard to my mother which said simply, 'The catwalk is built over a swimming pool. Need I say more!'

Nevertheless, I needn't have worried. The evening was perfect and the showing a glittering success. As I showed my final evening dress and removed the great billowing coat nonchalantly, part of it trailed off into the water behind me. But this apparent negligence and disregard only seemed to add to the pricelessness of my ensemble.

During the show I had noticed one table particularly because seated at it there were three oil-sheiks wearing spectacular white headdresses and black and gold djelebas sweeping the ground. All three, wore very Western looking sunglasses. Their teeth gleamed white against their swarthy faces and they were fascinating in an age-old wickedly attractive fashion.

The following day all the mannequins went on a sight-seeing trip to the beautiful Roman ruins at Baalbek. I was escorted around the ruins by an American male who had latched on to me the very first day on board ship; a 'nice guy' called, of all things, Joe. He came from New York. On our way to Baalbek I happened to glance out of the rear window of the car and idly noticed a beautiful silver Aston-Martin not far behind. At Baalbek we hired camels, and ambled along on those strange moth-eaten looking creatures. The ruins were fascinating and very impressive but what impressed me most of all – and gave me a shock – was to see the same three sheiks standing coolly in the shade of one of the pillars.

We returned to Beirut and again I noticed the same chauffeur-driven Aston-Martin. By this time I was sure that it was following us. When we finally stopped off at the gold

market there was the omnipresent threesome again. By this
time I had confided my panic to Joe. I have never before felt
such comfort from being with a simple plain Joe from New
York. As we passed them they bowed and hissed and made
squiggly Arab noises and then followed on dutifully behind.
The gold market in Beirut is known to be a great place for
bargaining, but I certainly was not prepared for what followed.
We had been inside one of the tiny little shops and I had just
bargained for and bought, all by myself, a beautiful little gold
ring. Outside the shop a liveried chauffeur doffed his cap and
handed an envelope to my escort. The three oriental
gentlemen were seated at a café table a few yards away
sipping the customary Turkish coffee. The fattest one stood
up and bowed as I glanced across. The chauffeur waited. We
opened the envelope and I read over Joe's shoulder, 'Your
woman she is very nice. I pay you 25,000 dollars for her cash
on delivery!'

'Sold into a harem!' I whooped. 'How marvellous,' I
exclaimed to my astounded American friend. 'I've always had
a sneaking desire to be kept in a harem.' Joe was shocked,
flabbergasted by both the offer and my reaction, so I
hastened to add, 'Just smile nicely at them and say you'll
consider it.' Now it was Joe's turn. 'I stand to make quite a
bit from the deal, too,' he mused. Then I glanced again at the
fat sheik and his beady black eyes and knew that it was time
to make our exit. 'Come on, Joe, let's go,' I urged him.
However, Joe insisted upon following some sort of protocol,
mainly, I suspect, because he feared to have a bunch of Arabs
dogging his footsteps throughout the trip. So, taking a manly
breath, he went over and explained that he had not had this
woman for very long and that she was certainly not for sale
at any price. Meanwhile I hung about in the background and
tried to look subservient. They seemed to understand and
laughed uproariously, and then everyone shook hands all
round and we left.

The next day our beautiful blue-and-white Greek passenger-boat weighed anchor, and we set off to sail among the Greek Islands, then on to Istanbul. A really fabulous city. We had a cocktail party aboard the ship with many V.I.P. visitors from shore, including most of the Istanbul 'Jet Set' plus a rich collection of silk merchants and their wives. One of the silk merchants offered me a really marvellously well-paid job modelling exclusively for his silk-products company in Izmir. I must confess to having been tempted, but when I got back to Paris my friends talked me out of it. All the same, I felt that the offer had been a serious professional one and not just another white slave traffic deal; but one never knows. One of the disadvantages of being a woman. If I had been a man, I think I would have been a sailor. I love the excitement of exploring new frontiers to one's existance; both geographical and situation-wise. It's just that as a woman . . . but enough said. As a woman, one has less liberty to indulge in suspect adventures, and all the Womens Libs in the world will never change that one.

We finally arrived in Naples and thence on to Cannes. Anchoring out there in the bay was a terrific thrill. We came in by launch to do our last show, this time held at the Palm Beach Casino. It was our *grande finalè* and a great success. We followed it up with a lavish dinner and then I wandered off to try my luck at the tables. Lady Luck sat upon my shoulder and smiled down on every action I made. I think she did anyway. I remember trusting her to do just that, so much so that I didn't even take into account whether I was losing or winning. I just concentrated upon enjoying myself and, although the colour of my chips was changing, I had more or less the handful that I had started with. Anyway, I trusted Lady Luck to do my calculating for me and when I came to count my chips at the end of a very interesting evening, I was told that I was £400 up. A wonderful feeling of elation passed over me. I decided to invest this money in a childhood dream and to buy a horse. The next day when all was being packed and got ready for the return to Paris I mentioned my project to Pierre Balmain and he suggested that instead of going with them to Paris I should fly directly to England to exercise my fantasy; but on the strict understanding that I should be back in Paris in ten days time. Now there's a man, I thought as I boarded the plane bound for Southend in Essex, who understands the importance of dreams. So much so in fact that he had built a whole multi-million-pound business around them. Of course he understood!

Having arrived back in England I telephoned my sister Diana, and after the preliminary squeals of sisterly greeting, she and husband Tom arrived in their car to take me home. The horse we bought was a beautiful dappled grey gelding which we named Samuel Beckett after the Irish Nobel Prize winner. It was a beautiful and solemn moment. Diana promised to take good care of him and I flew back to Paris in time to keep my promise.

When I arrived back I discovered that all my clothes and jewellery had been stolen. Hen and Fifi were moving house as our lease was up on the flat. So everything of mine had been packed in suitcases, and left with the downstairs neighbour. When I came to claim my things I discovered to my dismay that the suitcases were empty. It was a lamentable home-coming. Henrietta was for calling the police immediately, but I thought that we should perhaps wait and do some detective work ourselves first. Felicity just gasped and kept wailing, Oh Val, all your diamonds', until I mentioned to her as gently as I could that just one of my dresses was equal to all the paste glitter which I had lost put together. 'Bijoux Burma' while expensive by normal reproduction standards, doesn't in fact compare to an original *Haute Couture* creation. It was in fact our downstairs neighbour who did the detective work for us.

He had been absent for a weekend, and being a philan-thropist had lent his flat to two homeless girls upon whom he had taken pity. It sounded a little mythical if not mystical but he assured us that it was true. Now he had tracked them down to an address in Pigalle, so we all drove over there. It was about 10 p.m. when we found the address in the rue Blanche. The house belonged to a theatrical couple who had let their maid's room to two young girls recently; but they had become rather suspicious of them when they saw the large wardrobe of expensive *couture* clothes which seemed also to be much too large for them. In consequence they had notified the police, and a specialist in juvenile crime was waiting there when we arrived. It was all rather like a scene from Maigret. We climbed up a dark spiral staircase at the back of the courtyard to where the maids rooms were, on the 7th floor. Typical underside of French life; dreary brown-and-cream peeling paintwork, dirt and squalor. There was nobody in the room when we knocked, but the door was open and we all walked in. There were all my clothes, lying in crumpled heaps on the bed, jewellery scattered around the room, and belts, shoes and handbags galore. I felt awful. Somehow I didn't want to touch them and in fact didn't care to claim anything. Just then footsteps sounded outside on the stairs, and presently a girl of about sixteen with tear-stained cheeks walked in, wearing a little navy Lanvin suit of mine and a necklace and matching bracelet that an ex-boyfriend had given me, and carrying one of my handbags. She had even called herself Valerie. She was followed by two hard-faced French plain-clothes detectives and an elderly, matronly-looking woman. My first reaction was to leave them all, and to let the girl keep the property, everything — forget it — but since by now the authorities were involved they made her give everything back and then took her off into custody. She turned out to be a minor who had run away from home to seek adventure in the big city. She too had probably dreamed of being a model one day. For some it's just roulette and blind trust. For others the game rather resembles Russian Roulette. It's not a good way to play.

Owing to my show-business background it had always been a thing with me never to miss a show if I can possibly help it. I will go on even if I am half dead from exhaustion or have a raging toothache/headache/backache/broken neck etc. I always feel that at least just for three minutes – which is about as long as it takes to show a dress usually – I can get off my hands and knees, squeeze out that extra effort, and standing erect, radiate in the face of mundane adversity. Although I have often been criticized for being a congenital latecomer, and though I have given some people a few nasty moments, I don't believe I have ever missed a show or an entrance in my life. Once when we were all scheduled to go on a trip to Italy to do a show we were given a rendezvous at the Gare de Lyon for 7.30 p.m. The train left at 8 p.m. After spending two whole hours locked solid in a Parisian traffic jam that would make the London equivalent seem like Le Mans, I arrived in time to see the tail of the train just disappearing around the bend. It was a nasty moment and I could imagine the remarks of Balmain, Eric and the mannequins as they sipped their champagne suppers, and snuggled into their 1st class sleepers. So I determined to make that show in Italy come hell or high water. There was another train leaving at 11 o'clock, though not an express and without a 1st class sleeping car. I booked a ticket to Torino (Turin) and paid for it with my one and only 100 franc note. I had no other cash as I had not anticipated spending anything on myself. However, I sent a telegram to the rest of the party advising my time of arrival and requesting someone to pick me up at the station and to drive me on to the casino where the show was to take place. It was pouring with rain in Paris and I had begun to develop a really streaming cold. Perhaps it was just as well, however, for the couchette which I had hired turned out to be a compartment shared with two men. I was nervous, to put it mildly, and lay awake in the top bunk all night long waiting for either of them to make a false move and expecting one of them to reach for a meat axe or start growing fangs at any minute. However, my nose was bunged up and I snorted and sneezed all the way. I should think the sounds would probably have deterred the most depraved sex maniac in any case. Unless he were a nose man. The following morning the train stopped on the side of a mountain somewhere and everyone got out. It was some kind of a border halt, and a sleepy customs-officer eyed me and my eyelashes and my passport suspiciously and then pinched my bottom and yawned as Italians are apt to do. I'm not sure which one of us he thought was dreaming. The early morning mist swirled about my knees as I sat upon my suitcases and waited for another train to take me on to Turin. All the other passengers seemed to have disappeared, heaven knows where as there did not appear to be anywhere to disappear to, apart from a few cottages and a mountainside.

Eventually a small diesel coach arrived and took me on to Turin. After stopping at every station *en route* we arrived at about 2.15 in the afternoon. I donned my dark glasses and prepared to make a star-like entrance for the benefit of the reception committee which I felt certain would be awaiting me, with a fast car warming up ready to whisk me off to the casino. The only occupants of the platform, however, were a few ogling porters, some sleepy Italian peasants, and a great statue of the Virgin Mary. Gradually my predicament dawned upon me. I had no money, no idea of where I was supposed to go, and no *parla Italiano* either.

After wandering round the station for a while contemplating my situation, I came upon a map and discovered that the casino was in a tiny village in the mountains, quite a considerable journey from Turin. After a great deal of arm-waving and pointing, winking and pinching from a group of operatic tenors, I discovered that there was a bus going in the direction of Timbuctoo and leaving from the front of the station in thirty minutes. I decided to get aboard and then try to explain my case to the conductor. Perhaps I could pay at the other end. Or perhaps I could give my name and address or something. What an optimist! The bus rattled off full of fat ladies, kids and a few chickens. I squeezed in beside an old man with a nicotine-stained moustache and a sack with something moving inside it on his lap. The bus jolted into movement and we were off.

A fine way for a star mannequin to arrive at a show, I thought to myself. A man with a small flat cap balanced on top of a large fat head and a face like a dish of canneloni came around for the fares, and I explained as best I could that I was entirely without the essential in an essentially materialistic world, but that everything would be alright if I could just arrive at 'Timbucktooia' (the actual name of the place still eludes me). With the complacent smile of the truly dedicated obstructionist he responded with reams of incomprehensible but evidently negative Italian, and escorted me off at the next stop where he handed me over to the Carabinieri. The Carabinieri were much more interested in me than they were in the bus conductor's story. They accordingly arrested me, and hovered around grinning and winking and patting their revolvers like a bunch of dangerous small boys. One of them spoke a little French and so once again I told my story explaining that I simply had to get to Timbucktoo and a half before 7 o'clock that evening as I had a very important fashion show to do. He then relayed this on to his mates, who were fascinated. The time was then about 4.30 in the afternoon. I shall always be grateful to the Italian Carabinieri for what happened next. We all piled into a tiny black-and-white Fiat, me in the middle flanked by two middleweight champion spaghetti eaters. Then we literally took to the hills at a horrific pace, siren blaring, chickens and children scattering out of our path, round and round and through some ghastly mountain passes. As we sped round the semi-circular lip of a ravine one of my escorts delightedly pointed out shrines erected to the blessed Virgin where various victims had been promoted to glory on that spot. I could see some of the mangled wrecks below peeping through the weeds.

Three hours later we drove up to the elegant Baroque entrance of the casino in the Italian Alps. The car screeched to a standstill, siren still blaring as we all piled out and rushed inside like characters from a Thurber vignette. I had made it. Dashing directly backstage to the *cabine* I was greeted by Monsieur Balmain. I decided to play it cool, and slowing down to a breathless saunter I murmured '*Bonjour Monsieur*' and, though shaking with nerves, with calculated calm I continued to my place at the dressing table. But Balmain managed to 'out cool' me. There I was arriving in the nick of time accompanied by a bunch of crazy volatile Italian policemen, having had a perfectly frightful journey and feeling like death warmed up and all he said was 'Tiens! Te voila toil. Mettez-vous ca.' (Ah, there you are. Here, put this on.) And I was into my first dress and making my entrance, bang on time.

The sort of travelling I like best is when I am occasionally free to travel down to somebody or other's country home. Some friends of mine live in a most beautiful twelfth-century Château in the Dordogne. Every year during the month of October they invite friends down to help with the grape harvest or *vindange* as it is called in French. A real Tom-Jones-type affair it is too, by which I mean bucolic à la Fielding, rather than 'yay yay' à la his Nevada-based namesake. The fellow house-guests are usually varied, with a goodly sprinkling of American bankers and other business-men letting down their uptight hair whilst sipping Armagnac and squeezing bunches of grapes and good red earth between their spreadeagled toes; getting back to nature in a painless fashion and one which forever seems to keep its charm. Mother Nature seems to keep us on a long piece of string and as we get further away so the compelling urge to return intensifies.

On one of my latter visits I was down on my knees clutching a pair of secateurs and snipping away at a particularly luscious bunch of grapes when my hand collided with another hand going after the same bunch. The vine shook and then parted and a face appeared and hissed, 'Scorpion'. This really freaked me and I leapt up. 'How did you know I was a Scorpion,' I asked. He was about six foot seven, with a long pointed aristocratic Spanish face that reminded me of an El Greco.

'You got me with the secateurs so I guessed you might be the type', he said, exhibiting a pure hundred per cent American accent and a bloody finger. It dawned upon me that he must be the Spanish marquis who was so terribly rich and terribly handsome and terribly eligible that everyone felt certain he would make a perfect mate for me. Don Luis was his name. I can't say I didn't find him rather fascinating. Well, from there we took off on this whole rift that sent me skyrocketing half way round the world.

First we made the grand tour of his domains in Spain taking in several *casas* and a forest or two. And then finally came the inevitable meeting with the rest of the family. They were pretty sceptical of any other attractions outside their own family values. They were a strange mixture of hard-hitting Americanos and simple-minded Spaniards, with all the complexes of the two nationalities. Don Luis combined the two sets of qualities within himself. At times he could be a simple Spanish boy showering me with *piropos* and charm, and then the next moment he would be like a typical Brooklyn American, with all the chat and witticisms. He had all the antique elegance of the old Spanish families combined with the brash know how of a Californian. He was terribly good at everything such as flipping a pack of cards like a Mississippi gambler or riding a horse or dancing a Paso Doble like a Toreador.

Was this the man of my life? I asked myself. Would he be the one to 'take me away from all this' – provided that I wanted to be taken away from all this! Certainly he would be able to keep me in a manner to which I had become rather accustomed and certainly his attentions gave every sign that he was entirely smitten. I was showered with gifts and bouquets of flowers. But was it *me* he was fascinated by, or that exterior high-fashion-model image. Perhaps he was the all-time champion, ace game-player of the western world. I felt way out of my depth, but it was rather exciting too.

One night after our return to Paris from Spain I borrowed a gorgeous orange-and-gold brocade evening dress and a black diamond mink coat, and put on my 'diamonds'. A party of us were going to dine at Maxims. Maxims is decorated in its original Art Nouveau style and this went perfectly with my dress.

Since money was of course no object, I decided to order the most *haute cuisine* thing that I could find on the menu, beginning with caviar followed by Foie gras et cetera. The waiter appeared bearing a silver platter and a whole lot of machinery, and busily stirred basted and set fire to something which he then presented to me with a tremendous flourish and 'Ta Rah'.

There, upon a plate, lying on their backs, were what looked like two tiny larks bathed in a fancy *haute cuisine* sauce. So this was 'Caille' (à la Maxim). They were certainly beyond the stage where artificial respiration would have helped, but I couldn't bring myself to eat another morsel and took a swift gulp of Dom Perignon to fortify myself instead. Why hadn't somebody warned me? Just at that moment the band started playing tangoes, whereupon Luis turned out to be a tango virtuoso and we leapt, dipped and slid around the floor like Ginger and Fred. Even Bing Crosby and his wife, who also happened to be dining there that night, cleared a path for us. That road to Morocco was never like this and Bob Hope couldn't have told a more painful joke than the one I was attempting to suppress. Nevertheless I began to enjoy myself again. Maxims is many things, but it is not exactly the most swinging joint in town. Many would consider it rather old and staid. However, we had a wonderful evening since no place is more important than who you are with.

On our way home in a taxi I suddenly noticed that my diamond bracelet was missing. We retraced our steps, and even returned to Maxims. But there was no sign of it and I concluded that some Arsene Lupin jewel thief had also been amongst the crowd that night, and what with all my mink and jink, I must have been taken for real! Soon Don Luis had returned to San Francisco, and a whole stream of correspondence and transatlantic telephone calls began to flow. My life returned to normal – at least as normal as it ever could be, working for Balmain.

November and St. Catherine's day arrived. St. Catherine is the patron saint of all spinsters, and in particular of those unmarried girls who work in the *couture*. No work is done on the Feast of Saint Catherine, but each *atelier* and even the *cabine* is transformed into whatever theme has been chosen: a Fairy castle, an Arabian dream, or even the Wild West. All the little seamstresses dress up in costumes made by themselves, and there is food and lots of booze. The festivities begin at the unearthly hour of 10 a.m. and continue far into the night ending with a ball, or if you prefer, dancing to an accordian. There is something uniquely French about it all. On this day the Streets of Paris, especially around the eighth arrondissment, are usually full of strange characters, for later on it is open house and the feasters from Dior and Givenchy down the road pay a visit, and vice versa.

This is also, of course, the time of Halloween. Don Luis having returned to the States as mentioned I was beginning to feel rather lonesome, and I was invited to a party given by some American film people who were working on a Liz Taylor film. Balmain's assistant, Eric Mortensen, was also invited, with his friends Jacques and the countess. We finally decided to all go together. The theme of the party was naturally Witches and anything macabre. I wore a black lace dress with a jagged hemline. I freaked out my hair till it looked about a foot high. Then I put green eye shadow on my lips and pink lipstick on my eyelids. The effect was quite unnerving. Eric was dressed appropriately as the Prince of Denmark. The countess was another witch, while Jacques merely daubed tomato ketchup all over his evening dress shirt and went as 'a victim'.

The party was held in a large old empty house somewhere outside Paris. The trouble was that we lost the way and had to stop and ask directions from a gibbering passer-by. What's more, Jacques insisted upon getting out of the car to do so. . . . But the party when we eventually arrived was terrific. The Burtons and Warren Beatty were alleged to have been there too, but since everyone was in disguise this may or may not have been true. Anyway I was there, which is about as much as anyone could say. Fancy dress seems to give one an anonymity which encourages liberty of action, and we all cut loose and enjoyed ourselves tremendously.

Balmain and Eric always take a friendly interest in all our love affairs, especially if *he* happens to be very wealthy and therefore very chic. Eric also loves to give advice upon handling men, and every week asked me if I had had news of the marquis. So when one day towards Christmas a letter arrived with an invitation and a return ticket to San Francisco, he too was overjoyed.

Christmas and New year in California were memorable occasions. Don Luis and I drove in his convertible Rolls-Royce Silver Cloud along the gorgeous scenic coast-road, El Camino Real, from San Francisco to Los Angeles, where we were to spend Christmas at the home of his brother Alfonso and his beautiful wife Ludmilla. It felt very strange to be away from England at this time of the year, and to be among those sinister shiny black Christmas trees, laced with the bright Californian sunshine. The plastic reindeer on the roofs, covered with polystyrene snow, did nothing to dispel my feelings of homesickness.

Americans seem so busy doing things all the time and to work so hard at their recreations. Perhaps it is all the vitamins they take. However, I was suffering from a bad case of 'jet lag', and most of the time had a hard time just keeping my eyes open. I could have slept for days, but there didn't seem to be enough time for sleeping.

Being a Paris model, I found myself up against all kinds of scrutiny, with reactions ranging from gushing admiration to subtle claw-scratching. Ludmilla's greeting rang in my ears for quite a while: 'How do you do Valerie. I do hope you are going to change your clothes at least five times a day, so that we can all get a look at a Balmain model's wardrobe.' Oh God! I thought, what a busman's holiday.

Over Christmas dinner she had another go. Apparently I had picked up the wrong fork with which to eat the deeply-frozen hors d'oeuvre. I felt like asking for an ice-pick instead.

'Oh Valerie, how dare you use the wrong fork,' she said.

'Oh Ludmilla, how dare you notice,' I countered.

A few family days later we all arose very early, donned slacks and sweaters and fur coats, for it is chilly at that hour even in Los Angeles, and took our places to watch that piece of genuine Americana, The Rose Parade. It was absolutely fabulous. High stepping drum majorettes, floats made entirely of flowers, cowboys, Indians, film stars, the lot.

Afterwards it is the tradition that people go visiting. But first my Ludmilla said she wanted to stop off home for a minute. She was gone for a good ten minutes while we all sat and waited outside in the car. Suddenly she reappeared wearing a ravishing cocktail dress and jewellery, and with her hair up.

'I just thought I would change into something simple for the afternoon,' she said creamily. 'Oh but don't worry, you look gorgeous just as you are.' She smiled sweetly as we drove off. I was wearing corduroy trousers, boots and a sheepskin coat. We made the rounds of at least six different homes, each one more elegant than the last and everybody dressed to kill, and me in my boots, coat and sweater.

Around midnight we arrived home again, and as we wished each other goodnight Ludmilla said contentedly, 'Oh I hated to do that to you, Valerie!' I hadn't realised that my coming had meant so much to her. I only wanted to be happy and to live out my fairy story. I loved Don Luis on his white charger. How could I possibly explain this to her; I wasn't there to challenge anybody, I was merely following a star.

But my American trip wasn't all like that. I did meet quite a few very far in, far out, just plain nice people. Above all, I discovered the very real concern that all Americans share for their country and their tremendous enthusiasm for practically everything. Very refreshing after that other, older-style, European cynicism that Ludmilla had inherited. People are so open and friendly, and as far as New York was concerned it reminded me of the kind of friendliness that existed between people in London during the blitz.

Don Luis practised law in San Francisco, which is such a beautiful cosmopolitan city. It was rather like stepping right into a T.V. serial *a la* Perry Mason or "The Defenders" and it was amusing to listen to all the common chat about 'extradition orders' subpoenas and other such Bogartian jargon, but in my twilight daze I found it difficult to catch on quickly to what people were talking about, in spite of some well-meant advice from an American girl-friend to 'read Time Magazine every week so that you will have something to talk about with men!' Mind you, some of the locals in Frisco had a hard time understanding me too, until I learnt to say 'Sudder' instead of 'Sutter' Street, and 'budder' instead of 'butter'.

Don Luis was always very busy with his work and consequently I saw little of him after Christmas. One day he confided in me his theory that in order to make a successful man-woman relationship, you have to play hard to get. I concluded that this must be the reason he was so occupied all the time with his work. Therefore, I decided to become even harder to get, if that was the name of the game, and instead of staying on in California, a plan which we had both considered, I decided on the spur of the moment to head back to Europe. At least perhaps I would be able to sleep once again when I got back to my natural time cycle!

We remained the proverbial 'good friends' in spite of it all; amen.

9

"AND THEY LIVED HAPPILY EVER AFTER"

I was three days late for the start of the new fittings for the summer collection. Balmain was not in a very good mood as he had not yet found the line, and a pall was hanging over the House. This was not the moment to cross him, accidentally or otherwise. I crept into the studio and sat down to await my fitter, hoping that my absence had not been too conspicuous. But Balmain knew I was there and came and stood in the doorway to the inner sanctum, looking distinctly ominous. Attack was the best line of defence I decided, so I leapt up, rushed over, and kissed him on both cheeks. 'Happy New Year', I wished him, genuinely and warmly. What could he say? Fortunately our patron has a fabulous sense of humour.

Apart from all other considerations, however, it is quite a touchy moment – that first impression that one makes each new season. Very often upon that first impression depends whether one is in favour or out of favour as a mannequin. You may have been star mannequin last season and had more than twenty dresses in your collection, but this season it is quite possible that the powers-that-be will decide that your arms are too fat or your walk all wrong or that your look has just plain had it. Should this happen you could find yourself out in the cold, so it is important to make a good impact at the beginning of each season. Mine had been anything but that, but my alchemy must have vibrated in the right fashion.

There had been a few changes in the *cabine*, and one American girl had been replaced by a Hungarian. 'We just couldn't take that smile any longer dear,' Eric explained as being the cause for her absence. Also, a Danish model had been replaced by a German. 'It was simply not possible to fit her,' said Eric, 'she had such peculiar hip bones.'

So it is very important to try to change your look every season too, and to conjure up an aura that will, hopefully, inspire the maestro once again. 'New each morning' that beautiful Biblical expression, used to be my motto at such times, though it becomes hard to sustain after things get going. It tends to become a little more like the Thousand and One Nights; and morning just a blur away.

Towards the end of a season mannequins come round applying for jobs. They are put through their paces in just the same way as I was upon that first fateful day, and I always feel for them at this moment and wonder if they are feeling anything like I did. Of course the established mannequins take great delight in observing, criticising and dissecting the newcomer from the secure perch of their elevated egos. With their feet up on the dressing-tables, lolling back in their chairs, they make the most of being on the inside looking out, for however long it lasts.

The fittings were eventually over, and Press Day came and went with its usual accompanying bout of hysteria verging upon insanity. In the spring a whole spate of trips commenced, and we travelled all over Europe.

Meanwhile at home things were not quite the same either. Henrietta had returned to London to marry her stockbroker fiancé. She had had a fashionable wedding in the Guards Chapel. Fifi had also decided to leave Paris and to go back to London in order to work for Norman Hartnell, having acquired even more allure and sophistication from her Parisian episode, plus lots of Lanvin clothes and shoes and Chanel handbags. It had been a sad parting, and we vowed that we would all get together again some day and maybe show off our kids to each other and reminisce. On our way to the station in the taxi, Felicity kept saying, 'Just think Val, if it hadn't been for you none of this would have happened.' This was true I suppose, and I think she had really enjoyed her sojourn in Paris. But she was not at all interested, as I was, in becoming internationally oriented nor even a cosmopolitan European, and her French never did progress beyond 'Ooh la la'. In fact she had 'Margate' written all through her just like a stick of rock. I missed her an awful lot.

As for myself, I stayed on and on and on; and what had been originally planned as a three-month jaunt to gain a little chic in order to return to London and to get the plum modelling jobs, turned out to last for three years. Life, in fact, had become much too exciting in Paris for me to return to dear dull old London whose 'swinging' scene had lulled me to sleep. I was even getting used to the French manners, so different from that excessive English politeness and that rather diffident approach. English people generally find the direct and seemingly aggressive attitude of the French hard to take. It often seems just plain rude to them.

I also enjoyed what struck me as the unprofessionalism of the Paris show-modelling scene. It is really much less organised than in London or New York. Models work without agents, an unheard-of thing in New York or London. Mannequins get jobs by being in the swim and keeping their ears open for what auditions are being held. This does make for rather a *cliqué* group which is always working, where things are passed on to the girls that are liked. But once you are in, you are O.K. Some girls do get mean, and are afraid to pass on a titbit in case it makes too much competition for them; but 'do as you would be done by' is my philosophy and it generally pays off too. Once you do one freelance job it generally leads to others and this snowballs onwards. I much prefer this method, though of course one does have to fight for one's money, something an agent would normally do for one. There is quite a lot of exploitation of inexperienced mannequins too. There have been several girls who from time to time have tried to start a union of mannequins. The idea is a sound one; but trying to organise women into a body, and especially mannequins, is rather like attempting to create a Venus de Milo from the nebulous perfumes of a witches' brew. And besides, the French were always so busy trying to keep foreign girls from taking jobs from French girls.

It seems to me that the only sort of social trends that appeal to the French are those that unite them against the perpetual invader. Apart from this, they are the most anti-organisation individualists that one could find in this ready-to-wear, pre-packaged world.

Hamburg, Madrid, Rome. That spring we made these, and quite a number of other chic rendezvous as well. The Germans seemed to me to have an extremely big market for *haute couture*; they are very well-dressed and very fashion-conscious. There are, however, as in any generalisation, exceptions. One striking exception was an enormous Valkyerian Amazon whom I encountered while in full flight across the treacherously slippery ballroom floor of the Berlin Hilton. I was showing a gorgeous navy-and-yellow organza evening dress. Madame suddenly set off across the arena in the opposing diagonal, grimly bearing a plate of cream cakes (it was a tea time show). We met in the middle, both of us seemingly oblivious to the other's presence, and the scene had every potential for some Chaplin-type slapstick.

Now my German is strictly limited to two words, *Achtung* Spitfire. I found this a miraculously opportune moment to use them. They worked like a charm. She practically did a Zimmerman turn, and, banking abruptly, peeled off in the other direction, cream cakes and all.

A German T.V. company arranged a contract with Balmain

to do a whole series of films about the new collection. The shows were to be built around Hildegarde Kneff, the ex-film actress now turned singer. We eventually returned to France for the preparation of the T.V. shows, and we spent some lovely spring days filming out at Balmain's beautiful house overlooking the Seine at Croissy. The director worked against a backdrop of the magnificent glassed-in marble terrace, a priceless background of Art Nouveau vases by Gallé, and a collection of Tanagra statuettes and Greek vases that rivals any other in the world.

Wearing a luscious pale-lilac Balmain evening dress with rich jewel encrustations around the neck, Hildegarde Kneff was charming, sultry and starlike. She and her English husband invited some of us to dine at l'Orangerie one day after filming. After a delicious meal at this currently fashionable restaurant on the Ile St. Louis, we all went on to Chez Regine. Wigs were the rage that season and I had on a short curly one that looked rather like a coconut. It was frightfully hot on the dance floor (they sell more drinks that way) and while I was dancing 'Hands, Knees and Boomps a Daisy' (of all things) with Balmain, and exclaiming because of the heat, he took hold of my hair and lifted it right off! It was indeed very much cooler outside of that contraption and we laughed until the music ended.

The following day it was back to work again, filming on the Champs Elysées this time. There were two of us filming, myself and an American-Swedish girl from New York called Margit. She had won the sculpture prize at her college, and with the prize money she had come to Europe to search out her father in Sweden. Having a natural leggy elegance and that automatic professionalism that comes from being a New York girl, she applied for a job at Balmain and got it. She then spent the rest of her time *chez* Balmain worrying in case her brain might atrophy!

The weather was nice and cool and sunny and Margit and I

were ensconced in a beautiful horse-drawn carriage, trotting down the Champs Elysées, whilst a cameraman, clinging perilously to the edge of the open carriage, filmed the scene. At a given signal, each of us in turn was supposed to stand up in the jolting carriage, remove the coat elegantly and show the dress. I was wearing a misty grey-and-white sealskin maxi coat over a smart little white wool crêpe. Margit had on a chic little red wool outfit trimmed with black leather.

It took most of the morning to get the shots. Filming always takes an interminable time. During a break for a camera reload we decided to go and have a coffee at a nearby pavement café. We chose a table right in front so that we could watch the people, and relaxed there sipping Cointreau in our full make-up and expensive clothes. To add to our un-girl-next-door look we were both wearing sunglasses to cover up our false eyelashes and also because of the bright spring sunshine.

It was May once more and the chestnuts were in blossom. Back and forth went the electric springtime throng. This was the same café where three years ago I had sat waiting for Felicity on our first day in Paris. Much water had passed under the bridge since then. Many things had happened. Paris was no longer the exotic mystery that it had been. I felt myself to be much a part of the scene now. I belonged. I was a Parisian. I sipped my Cointreau contentedly and thought of the lines from a poem, 'God's in his heaven, All's right with the world.'

Suddenly I gripped Margit's arm as a tall figure materialised from the sea of unknowns. There was something familiar about him.

'What's the matter?' asked Margit.

'I'm sure I know that man,' I said. My voice sounded a long way off to me. I was elsewhere, lost in a mental flashback of images and trying to find the correct combinations to slot into my cerebral computer. The vibrations were very strong. I muttered incomprehensibly, 'London. I was an art student. He was a poet. It's so long ago. I was crazy about him. Fairy stories. He was always telling me to believe in fairy stories.'

'Well go after him then for Chrissake!' said Margit.

But I was too timid, and whilst I had been losing precious minutes trying to pluck up the courage he had gone past, and now all I could see was his back disappearing into the crowd. I no longer felt sure. 'But it might have been him,' a voice whispered insistently inside of me. I was surprised to notice that I was trembling with nerves or what may have been perhaps simple frustration at my lack of courage.

'I should have made sure,' I said to Margit.

'You sure as hell should,' she replied, 'now you'll never know. I hate uncertainty!' she added, 'It's not good for that clear unworried expression.'

I started to tell Margit a little about my past life in London, and about this boy I used to know who lived in a boat and wrote poetry and kept an Alsation dog named Sally, and who came to Paris eventually. He had become fanatically convinced that he had to start an English Language Theatre there. I had noticed something about him in the newspapers fairly recently when he had won much acclaim for an English production of Samuel Beckett's *Endgame* at the Theatre des Champs Elysées. I had thought about him often, though it had never occurred to me that I would ever run into him again. The world is large and so is a big city. I wasn't even certain that it had been him, and now it was too late. The more I thought about it, the more I felt convinced that the Gods had been plotting the unpredictable together. I had been too slow in the uptake as usual. If it had been him it would have been such an occasion. We had had a lot of real childish fun together before cold professional reason had intervened to separate us.

Suddenly I saw him again. It *was* him. The same abstracted

interior gaze and seeming obliviousness to his surroundings. He was lost I could tell; though how one can get lost in the wide open space of the Champs Elysées was beyond me. It was him alright. 'Michael', I called, leaping up and running after him, all my chic Parisienne veneer thrown to the winds. 'Michael', I called.

He turned and stared blankly at me and for an awful moment I thought maybe he didn't remember me. At the same instant I trembled at the thought that perhaps I had made a terrible mistake and that this was some total stranger whom I was accosting. But he knew his name at least. 'You *are* Michael', I said anxiously. Then I remembered that I was wearing 'full schlep'. Just at that moment his eyes pierced the disguise and made the bridge from the old white art-school duffle coat to the now luxurious sealskin fur coat.

His face broke into a big warm broad grin. 'Val!' he shouted, opening his arms wide. I ran to him. And right in the middle of the Champs Elysées we stood there hugging each other, standing back and looking at each other, hugging each other again, and dancing around each other. We were children again, and the tears rolled down our cheeks, and we lived happily ever after. Ah yes, indeed. One should never stop believing in the reality of one's own personal fairy story.

We live upon a mountain top as high as high can be.